DRAGON FOOD

WHIMSICAL TREATS

DRAGON FOOD

70 LEGENDARY, MAGICAL, AND FANTASY-INSPIRED RECIPES

CAYLA GALLAGHER

Skyhorse Publishing

Skyhorse Publishing books may be purchased in bulk at special discounts for sales promotion, corporate gifts, fund-raising, or educational purposes. Special editions can also be created to specifications. For details, contact the Special Sales Department, Skyhorse Publishing, 307 West 36th Street, 11th Floor, New York, NY 10018 or info@skyhorsepublishing.com.

Skyhorse® and Skyhorse Publishing® are registered trademarks of Skyhorse Publishing, Inc.®, a Delaware corporation.

Visit our website at www.skyhorsepublishing.com.

10 9 8 7 6 5 4 3 2 1

Library of Congress Cataloging-in-Publication Data is available on file.

Cover design by Kai Texel
Cover photo by Cayla Gallagher
Edited by Nicole Frail

Print ISBN: 978-1-5107-7699-9
Ebook ISBN: 978-1-5107-7700-2

Printed in China

Once they all believed in dragons
When the world was fresh and young,
We were woven into legends,
Tales were told and songs were sung,
We were treated with obeisance,
We were honored, we were feared,
Then one day they stopped believing—
On that day, we disappeared.
Now they say our time is over,
Now they say we've lived our last,
Now we're treated with derision
Where once we ruled unsurpassed.
We must make them all remember,
In some way we must reveal
That our spirit lives forever—
We are dragons! We are real!

—Jack Prelutsky

Dragon Pull-Apart Cupcake Cake, page 149

CONTENTS

Icy Dragon Horns, page 123

INTRODUCTION

Welcome to *Dragon Food: 70 Legendary, Magical, and Fantasy-Inspired Recipes*! Within these pages, you'll embark on a culinary journey filled with whimsy and flavor as you explore the enchanting world of dragons!

From fiery jellies to magical popsicles, each recipe is crafted to capture the essence of these mythical creatures while satisfying your taste buds! Get ready to unleash your inner dragon slayer and delight your guests with these cute and delectable creations that are sure to spark joy and ignite your imagination.

So, grab your apron and join us as we bring the magic of dragons to your kitchen!

Instagram: @pankobunny
YouTube: @pankobunny
Facebook: @pankobunnycooking

Griffin Egg Nests, page 2

Enchanted Forest

GRIFFIN EGG NESTS

MAKES 10 NESTS

10½ ounces (300 grams) dark chocolate
2 cups granola with raisins, nuts, and seeds
10 cupcake liners
30 white candy-coated chocolate eggs
Gold metallic food coloring spray

1. Melt the dark chocolate by placing it in a microwave-safe bowl and microwaving for 30-second intervals until melted, stirring at each interval.

2. Add the granola to the melted chocolate and mix until the granola is evenly coated.

3. Line a cupcake pan with 10 cupcake liners. Spoon some granola into the base of the cupcake liner to create a base, then spoon more around the edges, creating a nest shape.

4. Place the muffin pan in the fridge or freezer until the chocolate has set, about 30 minutes.

5. Place the candy eggs on a sheet of paper towel and gently spray the gold food coloring onto just the tips of the eggs. Set them aside to dry.

6. Once the chocolate has set, peel the cupcake liners off of the nests. Fill the nests with the eggs and serve!

Edible Moss

MAKES ABOUT 3-4 CUPS OF MOSS

2 large eggs
2 tablespoons granulated sugar
2 tablespoons honey
6 tablespoons all-purpose flour
2½ teaspoons baking powder
Green food coloring

1. Place the eggs and sugar in a bowl and beat with an electric mixer until light and doubled in volume. Add the honey and mix until combined.

2. Gently fold the flour and baking powder into the batter until just combined.

3. Divide the mixture into 3 microwave-safe bowls. Add different amounts of green food coloring to each bowl and gently mix until just combined.

4. Microwave the bowls for about 1 minute, until it has bubbled and risen.

5. Flip the bowls upside down on a cooling rack and cool for 10 minutes. Then remove the cake from the bowls and cool completely.

6. Tear into your desired shapes and sizes!

Double-Headed Crispy Rice Dragon

SERVES 8-10

Body:
½ cup unsalted butter
10 cups mini marshmallows
1 teaspoon vanilla extract
Green food coloring
10 cups crispy rice cereal

Tummy, spikes, and wings:
3 tablespoons unsalted butter
3 cups mini marshmallows
½ teaspoon vanilla extract
Green food coloring
4 cups crispy rice cereal

Edible Embers (page 56), or red hard candy
4 candy eyes
Toothpicks
6 mini marshmallows

Cooking spray
4 lollipop sticks or skewers

Make the body:
1. Melt the butter in a pot over low heat. Add the mini marshmallows and mix until fully melted. Remove from the heat and add the vanilla extract and green food coloring. Add the cereal and mix well.

2. Allow the mixture to cool until it is easily handled. Spray your hands with cooking spray, and shape the mixture into the dragon's body, tail, legs, arms, necks, and heads. When creating the necks and heads, stick 2 lollipop sticks or skewers into the body, bend them at the "necks" and use them as internal support, shaping the cereal sculpture around them.

3. Place the body in the fridge to chill for about 30 minutes. This will help the head and neck stiffen and set.

Make the tummy:
1. Melt the butter in a pot over low heat. Add the mini marshmallows and mix until fully melted. Remove from the heat and add the vanilla extract and green food coloring. Be sure to dye it a darker green than the body. Add the cereal and mix well.

2. Allow the mixture to cool until it is easily handled. Spray your hands with cooking spray and stick it onto the tummy, the tail, and the tops of the heads.

3. Create 2 (3 × 3–inch) disks, and place them in the fridge until very firm. Use a sharp knife to cut them into wing shapes, then attach them to the dragon with toothpicks.

Finish:
1. Stick candy eyes to both dragon heads. The cereal mixture should still be sticky enough to easily attach them.

2. Stick the red embers onto the dragons' mouths to look like fire.

3. Use scissors to cut the mini marshmallows in half. Stick them to the dragon's front and back feet as claws.

4. Serve and enjoy!

Dragon Mud Print Cookies

MAKES 35 COOKIES

1½ cups all-purpose flour
½ cup cocoa powder
½ teaspoon salt
½ teaspoon baking powder
¾ cup unsalted butter, room temperature
¾ cup brown sugar
¼ cup granulated sugar
2 large egg yolks
1½ teaspoons vanilla extract
5 tablespoons milk (if needed)

Dinosaur toy

1. Preheat the oven to 350°F.

2. Place the flour, cocoa powder, salt, and baking powder in a medium-sized bowl and mix until combined.

3. In a large bowl, combine the butter, brown sugar, and granulated sugar. Beat with an electric mixer until light and fluffy. Add the egg yolks and vanilla extract and mix well.

4. Add the dry ingredients to the wet ingredients and mix until fully combined. If you find that the dough is too dry, gradually add up to 5 tablespoons milk, until the dough holds together and resembles cookie dough.

5. Roll the dough into 35 balls and place them on baking sheets lined with parchment paper.

6. Use your favorite dinosaur toy to press footprints into the center of each cookie. Place the baking sheets in the fridge for 1 hour to chill the dough. This will prevent the cookies from rising too much in the oven and ruining the footprints!

7. Bake the cookies for 9 minutes, cool completely, and enjoy!

Dragon Fossils

MAKES 3 FOSSILS

2 cups melted white chocolate
17 ounces (500 grams) chocolate cake
    (Griffin Cutout Sheet Cake, page 63)
1 cup frosting (from 3D Dragon Egg
    Cake, page 17)
3 cups melted dark chocolate

Dragon-shaped molds

1. Pour the white chocolate into 3 dragon-shaped molds. Place the molds in the freezer until the chocolate has fully set, about 30 minutes.

2. In the meantime, break the chocolate cake into fine crumbs. Add the frosting to create a cake pop dough! The cake should hold its shape when rolled into a ball.

3. Gently unmold the chocolate dragons and wrap them in the cake pop mixture. They don't have to be perfect circles—make them look as natural as possible!

4. Place the fossils on a tray lined with parchment paper and place them in the fridge until the cake is stiff, about 45 minutes.

5. Pour the melted dark chocolate into a large bowl and, working with one fossil at a time, coat in dark chocolate, then return to the tray and chill in the fridge until the chocolate has set, about 1 hour.

6. Have fun biting into a fossil and discovering that dinosaur you have found!

DRAGON OATMEAL

SERVES 2

1 cup old-fashioned oats
2 cups water
Pinch of salt
¼ cup coconut cream, plus extra for
   serving
1 fresh peach, peeled and diced
1 teaspoon matcha green tea powder
4 slices of banana
8 raisins
1 strawberry, sliced
½ green apple
Lemon juice

1. Place the oats, water, and salt in a pot and set to medium heat.

2. Stir constantly for 10 minutes, until the oatmeal has absorbed the water and softened. Add the coconut cream and mix well.

3. Set one third of the oatmeal aside. Add the fresh peach to the remaining oatmeal and then divide it between 2 bowls.

4. Add the matcha powder to the separated one third of the oatmeal and mix together. Spoon the now-green oatmeal into the other 2 oatmeal bowls to create the dragon's face and snout.

5. Use the bananas for the eyes, the raisins for the pupils and nostrils, and little slices of strawberry for the tongue. (See photo.)

6. Create the dragon's ears and horns with apple. (See photo.) Squirt some lemon juice on them to prevent them from browning. Enjoy!

Dragon Footprint Pie

MAKES 1 (9-INCH) PIE

Crust:
1 cup butter
2¼ cups all-purpose flour
1½ cups whole wheat flour
¼ cup granulated sugar
1 teaspoon salt
3 tablespoons ground flax seeds
1 cup ice water

Filling:
6 cups frozen raspberries
1 cup granulated sugar
6 tablespoons cornstarch
Juice and zest of 1 lemon
1 pinch salt
2 tablespoons unsalted butter
1 egg, beaten

Make the pie dough:
1. First, brown the butter. Place it in a pot and set it to medium-low heat. Heat it until it becomes a deep brown, stirring every so often. Pour it into a bowl and place it in the fridge until chilled and solid. You could also put it in the freezer if you're in a rush.

2. Combine both flours, sugar, salt, and flax seeds in a food processor. Add the chilled brown butter and pulse until the butter has been broken into pieces and well combined.

3. Transfer it to a large bowl and add the water gradually, until the dough comes together. It will

feel more like a bread dough than a pie dough, but this is okay!

4. Divide the dough in 2, wrap in plastic wrap, and chill in the fridge while you make the filling.

Make the filling:
1. Place the raspberries, sugar, cornstarch, juice and zest of a lemon, and salt in a large pot and stir to combine.

2. Set the pot to medium heat and cook until everything is combined and the filling is bubbling.

3. Remove it from the heat, add the butter, and stir to combine. Pour it into a bowl, cover with plastic wrap, and chill in the fridge until cooled to room temperature.

Assemble the pie:
1. Preheat the oven to 350°F.

2. Roll one half of dough out on a floured surface until it is about a 10-inch circle.

3. Gently place the dough into a 9-inch pie dish. Use a fork to pierce the surface of the pie crust. Trim off any excess crust.

4. Fill the crust with the cooled raspberry filling.

5. Roll the other sheet of dough out to a 10-inch round. Use a sharp knife to cut out dragon feet from the center of the circle. Gently place the sheet on top of the pie. Use a tiny amount of water as glue to stick the bottom crust to the top crust, then trim the edges of the top crust to look nice and clean.

(Continue on next page)

6. Use two fingers to crimp the pie crust edges, then brush the entire surface of the pie with the beaten egg.

7. Place the pie on a baking sheet and bake for 1 hour 45 minutes to 2 hours, until the filling is bubbling and the crust is very browned.

8. Cool the pie completely and serve with ice cream!

Matcha Dragon Doughnuts

MAKES 6 DOUGHNUTS

Doughnut batter:
1 cup all-purpose flour
1 tablespoon matcha green tea
    powder
1 teaspoon baking powder
¼ teaspoon salt
3 tablespoons unsalted butter, melted
¼ cup granulated sugar
2 tablespoons honey
1 large egg
½ teaspoon vanilla extract
⅓ cup + 1 tablespoon buttermilk
Cooking spray

Glaze:
12 mini chewy chocolate candies
    (e.g., Tootsie Roll)
6 chewy vanilla caramels
    (e.g., Werther's)
3 tablespoons whipping cream
1 cup confectioners' sugar
Brown, red, and green food coloring

Bake the doughnuts:
1. Preheat the oven to 400°F. Whisk together the flour, matcha green tea powder, baking powder, and salt in a small bowl and set aside. In a large bowl, combine the butter, sugar, honey, egg, and vanilla extract.

2. Add the buttermilk and mix until combined. Add the dry ingredients and milk until just combined—make sure not to overmix. Spoon

the batter into a piping bag and snip off the end, creating a large hole.

3. Spray a regular-sized doughnut pan with cooking spray. Bake for 7 minutes. Cool for 1 minute in the pan, then flip the pan over to remove the doughnuts and cool completely on a wire rack.

Make the candy dragons:
1. Create one dragon at a time. Unwrap and microwave 2 mini chocolate candies and 1 vanilla caramel for about 20 seconds. This will make both more malleable.

2. Use the chocolate candy to create the dragon's body, as well as the veins of its wings. Use the vanilla caramel to create the base of the wings. Stick the veins onto the caramel wings. If they're not sticking, very lightly wet the veins and use the wetness as glue.

3. Bend the wings and body so that they will sit nicely on the doughnuts.

Make the glaze:
1. Whisk together the whipping cream and the confectioners' sugar and whisk until fully combined.

2. Place a drop of brown food coloring, red food coloring, and green food coloring onto different spots in the glaze, and stir in just those little spots so that you have 3 colors in one bowl.

3. Dunk each doughnut into the glaze and twist a little bit, creating a swirl of all 3 colors. Return to the wire rack. Top with the dragon's body and wings and enjoy!

3D Dragon Egg Cake

MAKES 1 (6-INCH) CAKE

Cake batter:
1 cup unsalted butter, room temperature
2 cups granulated sugar
3 teaspoons vanilla extract
6 large eggs
3 cups all-purpose flour
1 teaspoon baking soda
1 teaspoon salt
1½ cups sour cream
1 cup melted white chocolate
Green food coloring

Buttercream:
2 cups unsalted butter, room temperature
1 teaspoon vanilla extract or seeds from 1 vanilla bean
5 cups confectioners' sugar
Green, black, brown, and blue food coloring
Metallic gold food coloring spray
Edible Moss (page 3)

Bake the cake:
1. Beat the butter and sugar with an electric mixer until pale and smooth. Add the vanilla extract and eggs one at a time, mixing with each addition.

2. In a separate bowl, combine the flour, baking soda, and salt. Add this to the batter in 2 additions, alternating with the sour cream. Add the melted white chocolate and several drops of green food coloring and mix well.

3. Spoon the batter into 3 greased and floured 6-inch round cake pans. Bake at 350°F for 30 minutes, or until a skewer inserted into the centers comes out clean. Cool completely.

Make the buttercream:
1. Beat the butter with an electric mixer until pale and fluffy. Add the vanilla extract and confectioner's sugar 1 cup at a time, beating with each addition.

2. Dye the buttercream a deep blue color.

Assembly:
1. Slice the tops and bottoms off the cakes to smooth the surface and remove any excess browning.

2. Stack the cakes and spread some buttercream between each layer. Carve the cake into an egg shape with a serrated knife.

3. Coat the cake in a thin layer of buttercream, called a crumb coat. This will catch any excess cake crumbs. Chill the cake in the fridge for 20 minutes.

4. Place the buttercream into a piping bag fitted with a large, round piping tip. Pipe 3 to 4 dollops on the top of the cake and use a cake spatula or knife to drag the dollop downwards, creating a scallop shape. Repeat with another row of dollops right beneath the scallop.

5. Return the buttercream to the bowl and add some green food coloring to create a forest green color. Return the buttercream to the piping bag without cleaning it—this will create a smoother transition between the blue and green shades. Create 3 more rows of scallops.

6. Return the buttercream to the bowl and add some brown food coloring. Return it to the piping bag and pipe another 3 to 4 rows of scallops.

7. Return the buttercream to the bowl one more time and add black food coloring, creating a very deep, green color. Pipe enough scallops to cover the rest of the cake.

8. Spray the cake with a light dusting of gold food coloring spray.

9. Serve the cake surrounded by Edible Moss for an earthy effect.

Dragon Tear Drops

MAKES 5 (2-INCH) DROPS

1½ cups water
¼ teaspoon + ⅛ teaspoon agar agar
1–2 drops liquid green food coloring
1 tablespoon granulated sugar
½ cup brown sugar
Dragon Scale Dust (optional, page 95)

Half-sphere mold

1. Place the water and agar agar powder in a pot and whisk together.

2. Set the pot to medium heat and bring to a boil. Boil for about 1 minute. The agar agar must be boiled in order to activate!

3. Remove the pot from the heat and add the green food coloring and granulated sugar. Whisk until the sugar has dissolved.

4. Place a half-sphere mold onto a tray and fill with the jelly mixture. Place in the fridge until set, about 30 to 45 minutes.

5. When ready to serve, heat the brown sugar in a pot until melted. Place a teardrop on your plate, sprinkle with some Dragon Scales if desired, and drizzle some brown sugar syrup on top.

Dragon Egg Cheese Balls

MAKES 3 (6-INCH-TALL) EGGS

Variation 1:
½ cup chopped apple
½ pound cream cheese, room temperature
¾ cup grated orange cheddar cheese
¾ teaspoon maple syrup
¾ cup pecans, finely chopped
1 cup grated Parmesan

Variation 2:
½ pound cream cheese, room temperature
1 cup grated orange cheddar cheese
½ tablespoon Dijon mustard
Pinch black pepper
½ cup pecans, finely chopped
1 cup sliced almonds

Variation 3:
½ pound cream cheese, room temperature
½ cup grated cheddar cheese (white and
   orange mix)
¾ cup goat cheese, room temperature
¼ teaspoon black pepper
2 cups mini gherkins

Crackers:
1 sheet (9¾ × 10½–inch) puff pastry

Make the cheese balls:
1. Mix all but the last ingredient for each variation together.

2. Dollop each mixture into the center of a large sheet of plastic wrap. Wrap the plastic wrap around the mixture and shape them into eggs. Place them in the fridge to stiffen, about 1 to 2 hours.

3. Roll Variation 1 in grated Parmesan. To decorate Variation 2, stick almond slices onto the egg starting at the bottom of the egg and working upward. For Variation 3, slice the mini gherkins diagonally into thin slices and slick them onto the egg, starting from the bottom and working upward.

Make the crackers:
1. Preheat the oven to 400°F.

2. Roll out a sheet of puff pastry to ⅛-inch thick. Cut out your desired shapes with a cookie cutter. Place them on a baking sheet lined with parchment paper. Place another sheet of parchment paper on top, then another baking sheet. The weight of the baking sheet will prevent the crackers from puffing up!

3. Bake the crackers for 10 to 15 minutes, until golden brown. Serve alongside the eggs and enjoy!

Dragon Sugar Cookies

ABOUT 18 COOKIES

Cookie dough:
2 cups all-purpose flour
¼ teaspoon salt
½ teaspoon baking powder
½ cup unsalted butter, room temperature
1 cup granulated sugar
Black food coloring
2 tablespoons milk
1 large egg
1 teaspoon vanilla extract

Royal icing:
⅓ cup warm water
2½ tablespoons meringue powder
½ teaspoon cream of tartar
4 cups confectioners' sugar
Orange, yellow, and black food coloring

Dragon-shaped cookie cutter

Bake the cookies:
1. Preheat the oven to 350°F.

2. Mix together the flour, salt, and baking powder. In a separate bowl, combine the butter and sugar and beat with an electric mixer until light and fluffy.

3. Add a couple drops of black food coloring to the milk, mix well, then add the milk to the butter mixture along with the egg and vanilla extract. Mix until well combined.

4. Add the dry ingredients to the wet and mix until well combined.

5. Shape the dough into a ball, wrap in plastic wrap, and chill in the fridge for 1 hour.

6. Roll the cookie dough out to ¼-inch thick and cut into dragons with a dragon-shaped cookie cutter. Transfer to a baking sheet lined with parchment paper and bake for 10 minutes, until the edges start to brown. Cool completely.

Make the royal icing:
1. Pour the warm water into a large bowl. Add the meringue powder and whisk for a couple seconds, until frothy. Add the cream of tartar and whisk again.

2. Add the confectioners' sugar in one addition and, using an electric mixer, beat for 10 minutes on low speed.

3. Dye one quarter of the royal icing orange. Leave about ⅓ cup of the remaining icing white and dye ⅓ cup black. Dye the remaining icing yellow.

Decorate:
1. Place the yellow icing in a piping bag fitted with a small, round piping tip. Pipe the outline of the dragon's body, minus the tummy, onto the cookies and immediately fill it in with more icing. Allow it to dry completely, about 30 minutes.

2. Pipe the dragon's wings with more yellow icing. Place the orange icing into another piping bag fitted with a small, round piping tip. Pipe the dragon's tummy and spots.

3. Use a toothpick to place a dollop of black icing onto the dragon as its eye and an even smaller dollop of white icing as the sparkle in its eye.

4. Let the cookies dry completely, about 2 hours, then enjoy!

Frozen Griffins

MAKES 2 GRIFFINS

1 banana
1 cup white chocolate chips, melted
1 cup semisweet chocolate chips, melted
¼ cup chocolate sprinkles
10 orange candy-coated chocolate chips
2 lollipop sticks
4 toothpicks

1. Cut a banana in half and stick both halves onto lollipop sticks, with the ends of the banana pointing upward.

2. Coat the bottom half of each banana with the melted semisweet chocolate chips, then roll it in chocolate sprinkles to look like fur.

3. Use the extra semisweet chocolate chips to create wings on a tray lined with parchment paper. Break one toothpick in half and build the wings on top of them. This will help them attach to the banana! Place the wings in the fridge to set while you continue decorating the griffins.

4. Coat the top half of the bananas with melted white chocolate chips. You can dunk the bananas into the white chocolate or spread it onto the bananas. While the chocolate is still wet, stick the orange candy-coated chocolate chips to the bananas to create the beak and the talons.

5. Use some extra chocolate to create the griffin's eyes and eye sparkle.

6. Once the wings have hardened, stick them into the back of the bananas.

7. Place the bananas on a tray in the freezer until the bananas have frozen, about 30 minutes. Then enjoy!

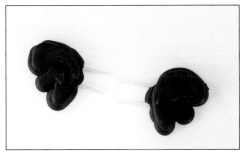
Step 3

Dragon Chow, page 55

Dragon's Lair

Dragon Egg Hot Chocolate Bomb

MAKES 1 BOMB

1 (3½ ounce/100 grams) dark or
   milk chocolate bar
1 tablespoon cocoa powder
2 tablespoons granulated sugar
1 tablespoon mini marshmallows,
   if desired
Edible glitter
Lemon extract
1–2 cups hot milk

Egg mold

1. Break the chocolate into small pieces and place it in a microwave-safe bowl. Microwave it for 20- to 30-second intervals, mixing at each interval. The chocolate can also be melted using a double-boiler.

2. Fill 2 cavities of an egg mold three quarters of the way full with the chocolate and gently rotate it so that the chocolate coats all sides. Place a sheet of parchment paper on your work surface. Turn the mold upside down and allow the excess chocolate to drip onto the parchment paper. Scrape the chocolate off the parchment paper and return it to your bowl.

3. Use the flat back of a butterknife to smooth the edges of the chocolate mold. Place the mold in the fridge for 20 to 30 minutes, until the chocolate has fully set.

4. Repeat steps 2 and 3 to create a second layer of chocolate. This will prevent the chocolate shell from breaking during unmolding and assembly. When smoothing the edges of the chocolate mold with the butterknife, ensure that the edges of the shell are 1 to 3 millimeters thick. This will allow both halves to securely stick together in the following steps.

5. Gently unmold the chocolate shells and rest them on a plate or on top of small glasses, which will support the egg shape very well and keep it from wobbling away.

6. Make the hot chocolate mix by combining the cocoa powder and sugar in a small bowl. Spoon some of the mix into one chocolate shell. You don't have to use all of the mixture. Add some marshmallows, if desired.

7. Re-melt some of the remaining melted chocolate and spread it onto the ridges of the filled shell. Place the other shell on top, press gently to seal, and place the hot chocolate bomb into the fridge for 10 minutes, or until the chocolate seal has set.

8. To decorate, combine some edible glitter and a couple drops of lemon extract on a small plate. Use a paper towel to dab the glitter and apply it to the egg in a splotchy pattern. Allow about 15 minutes for the glitter to dry.

9. To serve, drop the hot chocolate bomb into a mug of hot milk. Stir and watch the marshmallows appear!

Gummy Dragon Tongues

MAKES ABOUT 10 (2- TO 3-INCH) TONGUES

1 (3-ounce) box red JELL-O
1 (3-ounce) box orange JELL-O
3 teaspoons powdered gelatin, divided
2 cups boiling water, divided
Cooking spray

1. Pour the red and orange JELL-O into 2 separate bowls. Add 1½ teaspoons gelatin to each bowl and whisk together. Then add 1 cup boiling water to each bowl and mix very well.

2. Place the bowls in the fridge until semi-set, about 20 to 30 minutes.

3. Spray a 6 × 6–inch square pan with cooking spray.

4. Pour the red and orange semi-set JELL-O into the pan at opposite ends, creating an ombre effect.

5. Place the pan in the fridge for 2 to 3 hours, or until the jelly has fully set.

6. Gently unmold the JELL-O from the pan and cut it into tongue shapes. For an extra detailed tongue, trim the sides of the tongues so that they have a slight curve to them, along with a cutout down the center of the tongue.

BRIMSTONE BREAD

MAKES 12 BUNS

Bread dough:
3 tablespoons warm water
2½ teaspoons active dry yeast
Red and orange food coloring
¾ cup milk
2 large eggs
1 tablespoon vegetable oil
½ cup unsalted butter, melted
⅓ cup granulated sugar
2 tablespoons salt
2 teaspoons vanilla extract
4 cups all-purpose flour

Crackle topping:
½ cup unsalted butter, room
    temperature
⅔ cup granulated sugar
1 teaspoon vanilla extract
1 cup all-purpose flour
¼ cup cocoa powder

Make the buns:

1. Pour the warm water into a large mixing bowl and sprinkle the yeast on top. Allow the yeast to develop for about 5 minutes, until foamy.

2. Add a couple drops of red and orange food coloring to the milk, until it is a reddish orange color.

3. Add the eggs, oil, butter, sugar, red milk, salt, vanilla extract.

4. Attach a dough hook attachment (or knead with your hands) for a couple minutes, or until the ingredients have just started to be combined.

5. Add the flour and knead for 5 minutes at medium speed (or by hand) until the dough is nice and smooth. Kneading by hand may take a little longer.

6. Shape the dough into a ball and place it in a greased bowl. Cover with plastic wrap, place it in a warm spot in your kitchen, and allow it to rise until doubled in size, about 1 hour.

Make the crackle topping:

1. Place the butter and sugar into a large mixing bowl and beat with an electric mixer until light and fluffy. Add the vanilla extract and mix until combined.

2. Add the flour and cocoa powder and mix until it resembles cookie dough. If the dough is too dry, add a little bit of water or milk until it comes together.

3. Roll the dough into a ball, wrap in plastic wrap, and leave at room temperature until needed.

Shape the buns:

1. Divide the dough into 12 pieces and roll them into balls. Place them on baking sheets lined with parchment paper.

2. Working with one bun at a time, roll about 2 tablespoons of crackle topping into a ball, flatten it with your hands, and then place on top of the bun. Press it down lightly to ensure it is attached. Repeat with the remaining 11 buns.

(Continue on next page)

3. Use a sharp knife to cut a crisscross pattern into the crackle topping.

4. Cover the buns with plastic wrap, place them in a warm place, and allow to rise until doubled in size, about 30 minutes.

Bake:

1. Preheat the oven to 350°F.

2. Remove the plastic wrap and bake the buns for 18 to 20 minutes, or until they are just starting to brown.

3. Cool completely and enjoy!

Dragon's Breakfast

MAKES 1 (9 × 5-INCH) LOAF OF BREAD

Black bread starter:
¼ cup water
2 tablespoons bread flour
¼ cup milk

Dough:
½ cup warm milk
¼ cup granulated sugar, divided
2¼ teaspoons active dry yeast
1 large egg, room temperature
2⅔ cups bread flour
1 teaspoon salt
Black food coloring
¼ cup unsalted butter, room
    temperature
Milk (for brushing the dough)
Fried eggs
Paprika

Make the starter:

1. Place the water and flour into a small pot and whisk until smooth and well combined. Add the milk and whisk to combine.

2. Set the pot to medium heat and whisk constantly until the mixture resembles pudding.

3. Remove it from the heat, transfer to a bowl, and place a sheet of plastic wrap on top (while still warm!). Allow it to cool to room temperature. I've found that placing it in a glass bowl cools it down very quickly.

Make the bread:

1. Pour the warm milk and 1 teaspoon sugar into a large mixing bowl. Add the yeast, mix, and allow it to develop for 10 to 15 minutes, until bubbly and frothy.

2. Add the remaining sugar, egg, flour, and salt and mix together with a spoon or spatula until it just starts to combine.

3. Add several drops of black food coloring, then transfer to a stand mixer fitted with the hook attachment. Mix on low speed for about 5 minutes. You can also do this by hand on a floured surface, but it may take a little longer.

4. Add the butter 1 tablespoon at a time, mixing well with each addition. Then increase the speed to medium and knead for an additional 6 to 8 minutes, until the dough is smooth to the touch.

5. Cover the bowl with plastic wrap and allow the dough to rise until doubled in size, about 2 hours.

(Continue on next page)

6. Butter and flour a 5 × 9–inch loaf pan. Set aside.

7. Turn the dough out onto a floured surface and knead it a couple times until it deflates.

8. Divide the dough into 4 balls. Roll out each ball of dough into a 6 × 6–inch square.

9. Fold 2 opposite corners of the square inwards, so that the points meet in the middle. Then roll it into a log, starting at a pointed (unfolded) end. Pinch the seams to the seal the log closed and place it in the loaf pan, seam side down.

10. Repeat with the remaining 3 balls of dough.

11. Cover the loaf pan with plastic wrap and allow it to rise until doubled in size, about 1 to 2 hours.

12. Preheat the oven to 350°F.

13. Brush the top of the bread with milk, then bake for 30 to 35 minutes, until it is starting to brown and sound hollow when lightly tapped.

14. Allow it to cool in the pan for 15 minutes, then turn out onto a wire rack and cool completely.

Serve:
1. Slice the bread, toast, and top with a fried egg and a sprinkle of paprika.

Sword in Stone Cake

SERVES 6-8

Cake batter:
2 cups all-purpose flour
2 cups granulated sugar
¾ cup cocoa powder + extra for
   coating the pan
2 teaspoons baking powder
1½ teaspoons baking soda
1 teaspoon salt
1 cup milk
½ cup vegetable oil
2 large eggs
2 teaspoons vanilla extract
1 cup boiling water

Frosting:
9 ounces cream cheese, room
   temperature
1½ cups unsalted butter, room
   temperature
1 teaspoon vanilla extract
3 cups confectioners' sugar
Black food coloring

Sword:
1 (8-inch) lollipop stick
⅓ cup melted white candy wafers
⅓ cup melted brown candy wafers
Silver edible glitter
Lemon extract

Bake the cake:
1. Place the flour, sugar, cocoa powder, baking powder, baking soda, and salt in a large bowl and mix together.

2. Add the milk, vegetable oil, eggs, and vanilla extract and mix with an electric mixer until combined.

3. Slowly add the boiling water and mix until well combined.

4. Grease and flour 3 (6-inch) round baking pans but use cocoa powder instead of flour to coat the pans. This will keep the outsides of the cakes looking rich and chocolatey, instead of pale and floury.

5. Divide the batter evenly between the pans and bake at 350°F for 30 to 35 minutes, until a skewer inserted into the center comes out clean. Cool for 15 minutes in the pan, then turn onto a wire rack and cool completely.

Make the frosting:
1. Beat the cream cheese and butter with an electric mixer until pale and fluffy.

2. Add the vanilla extract and confectioners' sugar 1 cup at a time, mixing with each addition.

3. Dye the frosting gray with the black food coloring.

Make the sword:
1. Dip the lollipop stick into the white candy wafers and place it on a tray lined with parchment paper.

(Continue on next page)

2. Spread more candy wafers on top and above the lollipop stick, creating the blade. You will need 3 to 4 inches of lollipop stick available to stick into the cake.

3. Spread the candy wafers in two strokes, so that a ridge is created in the middle, mimicking a blade.

4. Use the brown candy wafers to create the base of the handle. Transfer the tray to the fridge until the candy wafers have fully set, about 15 minutes.

5. Place the remaining brown candy wafers into a piping bag fitted with a small, round piping tip. Pipe the details of the handle onto the sword.

6. Mix some of the silver edible glitter with a couple drops of lemon extract, until it looks like paint. Use a food-safe paintbrush to paint the silver onto the blade of the sword.

7. Return the sword to the fridge until ready to use.

Assembly:
1. Slice the tops and bottoms off the cakes to smooth the surface and remove any excess browning.

2. Stack the cakes and spread some buttercream between each layer.

3. Use a serrated knife to carve the cake into a stone shape.

4. Coat the cake in a thin layer of buttercream, then transfer it to the fridge to chill for about 15 minutes.

5. Cover the cake in a thick, generous layer of frosting, making lots of swirls to mimic rock.

6. Sprinkle some edible glitter on top of the stone, then insert the sword into the top of the cake.

7. Slice and enjoy!

Dragon Fire Balls

MAKES 3 LOLLIPOPS

¼ cup each red, orange, and yellow hard
   candy, crushed
3 lollipop sticks

1. Preheat the oven to 325°F.

2. Line a baking sheet with a silicone baking mat or parchment paper (Silpat is best here).

3. Create 3 ombre ovals with the crushed candy, starting with yellow at the base, then orange, and finishing with red at the top. They will spread in the oven, so be sure to leave a couple inches between them.

4. Place the baking sheet in the oven for 6 to 8 minutes, until the candy has melted.

5. Use a lollipop stick to blend the colors together within each flame and pull it upward to create the tongues of the fire. Work quickly because the candy will cool quickly!

6. Before the candy fully cools, stick a lollipop stick into each flame and allow them to cool completely, about 30 to 40 minutes.

Dragon's Treasure

MAKES ABOUT 4 DOZEN GEMS

2½ cups granulated sugar
1 cup water
1½ cups light corn syrup
Your choice of flavoring
Red, yellow, green, and blue food coloring

Gemstone molds
Cooking spray, if necessary

1. Set a pot over medium heat and add the granulated sugar, water, and light corn syrup. Stir with a rubber spatula until everything is melted and combined. Then increase the heat to medium high and attach a candy thermometer to the pot. Heat the sugar until it reaches 310°F.

2. Remove the pot from the heat and stir until it stops bubbling. Add 1 to 2 drops of flavoring and mix until fully combined.

3. Pour half of the candy into another pot. Dye one pot yellow and one pot blue. Pour the candy into your desired silicone molds. Add some red food coloring to the yellow candy and yellow food coloring to the blue candy to make orange and green candy. If the candy is starting to stiffen, simply turn the heat back on and allow it to melt. Pour the remaining candy into more silicone molds. NOTE: If using a silicone mold, you can pour the candy right in. If using a hard plastic mold, be sure to spray the mold with cooking spray first. This will prevent the candy from sticking.

4. Leave the candy at room temperature for 2 to 3 hours, until fully cooled and hardened. Then unmold and enjoy!

Dragon Tail Cinnamon Buns

MAKES 14 BUNS

Brioche:
⅓ cup whole milk, warm
2¼ teaspoons active dry yeast
5 eggs, divided
3¾ cups all-purpose flour, divided
⅓ cup granulated sugar
1 teaspoon salt
½ cup beet powder
1½ cups unsalted butter,
    room temperature, divided

Filling:
6 tablespoons brown sugar
3½ teaspoons cinnamon
1 egg, beaten
1½ cups unsalted butter,
    room temperature

Tails:
Red food coloring
2 cups modeling chocolate

Icing:
8 ounces cream cheese,
    room temperature
1½ cups confectioners' sugar
4 tablespoons milk

Make the Brioche:

1. Pour the milk, yeast, 1 egg, and 1 cup flour into the bowl of an electric mixer. Mix to combine, then sprinkle over another 1 cup flour. Let rise for 40 minutes.

2. Lightly beat the 4 remaining eggs, then add these to the dough along with the sugar, salt, beet powder, and 1 cup flour. Place these into a mixer fitted with a dough hook and mix on low speed for 2 minutes. Add ¾ cup flour and mix on medium speed for 15 minutes.

3. Reduce the speed to medium low and gradually add ¾ cup of butter. Increase the speed to medium high and beat for 1 minute, then reduce the speed to medium and beat for 5 minutes.

4. Place the dough in a large, buttered bowl and cover with plastic wrap. Let rise for 2½ hours.

5. Deflate the dough, then replace with plastic wrap, and place the bowl in the fridge. Chill in the fridge for 4 to 6 hours, or up to overnight.

6. Roll the dough out on a floured surface into a 20 × 20–inch square. Evenly disperse the remaining butter onto the surface of the dough, then fold the dough into thirds, like a letter.

7. Roll the dough out into a 20 × 20–inch square, then fold into thirds. Rotate the dough and fold into thirds again in the other direction to create a square. Wrap tightly in plastic wrap and place in the fridge for 30 minutes.

8. Combine the sugar and cinnamon in a bowl and set aside.

(Continue on next page)

9. Place the dough on a floured surface and roll into an 11 × 13–inch rectangle. Brush the surface with the beaten egg. Sprinkle the cinnamon sugar onto the dough, leaving the top quarter of the dough bare. Roll the dough into a log, starting with the cinnamon-sugar end and ending with the bare end. Wrap in plastic wrap and place in the freezer for 45 minutes.

10. Spread the final ¾ cup butter into a 9 × 13–inch rectangular baking dish.

11. Unwrap the log and slice it into 1½-inch thick buns, making 14 buns. Place the buns in the pan and let the buns rise at room temperature for 1½ hours.

12. Bake the buns at 350°F for 35 to 40 minutes, until golden brown.

13. As soon as the cinnamon buns are finished baking, flip them out onto a wire rack. Excess butter may drip out, so make sure to place some paper towel under the rack. Turn the buns right side up and set until slightly cool.

Make the tails:
1. Add some red food coloring to the modeling chocolate and knead until it is evenly red in color.

2. Divide the modeling chocolate into 15 pieces. Shape 14 pieces into arrow-like shapes. Use the remaining piece to add details and decorations to the tails.

3. 3. Place the tails at the natural end of each bun.

Make the frosting:
1. To make the icing, place the cream cheese in a bowl and beat with an electric mixer for 2 minutes, until the cream cheese is fluffy. Add the confectioners' sugar and milk and beat until combined.

2. Drizzle the icing on top of the buns and enjoy.

Fondant Dragon

MAKES 1 DRAGON

1 ounce (27 grams) white fondant
Green, blue, and black food coloring

Step 1

Step 2

Step 3

1. Set aside 0.02 ounces (0.5 gram) of white fondant and dye the remaining medium green.

2. Take 0.07 ounces (2 grams) of the medium green and dye it a deeper green with the blue food coloring.

3. Divide the medium green fondant in half. Use one half for the body. Use the other half for the head and other body parts.

Step 3

(Continue on next page)

4. Use a tiny touch of water as glue to attach the pieces to the head and body. Use the deep green fondant for the dragon's spikes and spots. Attach to the dragon with some more water.

5. Divide the white fondant in half. Use one half for the eyes. Dye the remaining white fondant black with food coloring. Use this for the pupils.

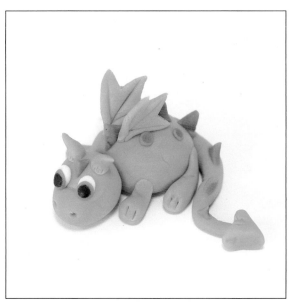

Step 5

Step 4

DRAGON IN A BLANKET

SERVES 2-3

14 ounces (397 grams) puff pastry
4 hot dogs
1 egg, beaten
Water
2 toothpicks
Ketchup and mustard, for serving

1. Preheat the oven to 425°F.

2. Roll the puff pastry out on a floured surface to 2 (6 × 13–inch) rectangles. Cut off a 2-inch strip from each long side, so that the rectangles become 4 × 13 inches. Save the excess dough.

3. Cut the hot dogs into 1-inch pieces. Divide the hot dogs evenly between the puff pastry rectangles, lining them down the middle of each rectangle. Leave about 1 inch of space above the hot dogs on one rectangle and one inch below them on the other. This is for the face and the tail.

4. Roll the puff pastry around the hot dogs and pinch them to seal. Gently transfer them to a baking sheet lined with parchment paper and pinch the two rolls together, creating a winding snake shape.

5. Shape one end into the face and one end into the tail. Use the excess dough to create the dragon's spikes, eyes, horns, nostrils, and tongue. Dip your finger in water and use the wetness as glue to attach these to the dragon.

6. Create the dragon's wings with more puff pastry, but instead of attaching them to the dragon, place them next to the dragon on the baking sheet. They will bake alongside the dragon.

7. Brush the dragon and its wings with the beaten egg and bake for 20 to 25 minutes, until golden brown.

8. Once the dragon has cooled, use toothpicks to attach the wings to the dragon, then slice and serve with ketchup and mustard!

DRAGON CLAW TRUFFLES

MAKES 18-20 (2-INCH CLAWS)

2 cups chocolate sandwich cookie
 (e.g., Oreos) crumbs
9 ounces cream cheese, room temperature
3 cups white candy wafers, melted
1 cup semisweet chocolate chips, melted
2 tablespoons cocoa powder

1. Place the cookie crumbs and cream cheese in a bowl and beat with an electric mixer until fully combined.

2. Divide the mixture into 18 to 20 pieces and shape them into claws. Place them on a plate lined with plastic wrap and refrigerate until firm, about 1 hour.

3. To add the coating to the truffles, place a truffle onto a fork and submerge it in the melted white candy wafers. Allow the excess candy melts to drip off, then return to the plate lined with plastic wrap.

4. Return them to the fridge to set, about 30 minutes.

5. Dip the widest ends of the claws into the melted chocolate chips and return to the plate. Use a food-safe paint brush to dust the claws with cocoa powder.

6. Chill the claws in the fridge until the chocolate has set, about 30 minutes. Then enjoy!

Dragon Scale Roll Cake

SERVES 6-8

Cake batter:
6 large eggs, yolks and white separated
Pinch salt
1 cup granulated sugar, divided
2 teaspoons vanilla extract
5 tablespoons unsalted butter, melted and cooled
1 cup all-purpose flour
Blue, pink, purple and black food coloring

Filling:
1 cup whipping cream, cold
2 tablespoons confectioners' sugar
1 teaspoon vanilla extract

Cream cheese frosting:
1½ cups unsalted butter, room temperature
9 ounces (250 grams) cream cheese, room temperature
1 teaspoon vanilla extract
3 cups confectioners' sugar
Blue, pink, and black food coloring
Silver edible glitter

Swiss roll pan

Make the cake batter:

1. Beat the 6 egg whites and salt with an electric mixer until soft peaks form. Add half of the sugar and beat until stiff, glossy peaks are formed.

2. In a separate bowl, beat the egg yolks and remaining sugar with an electric mixer until pale and doubled in volume. Gradually add the vanilla extract and butter and mix until well combined.

3. Add the flour to the batter in 2 additions, alternating with the egg whites. Divide the batter into 4 bowls and dye the batter black, pink, blue, and purple and gently fold to combine.

4. Line a Swiss roll pan with parchment paper. Dollop the batter into the pan, swirling with a knife to create a marble pattern. Bake at 350°F for 13 to 15 minutes, until the edges are golden.

5. Dust a large sheet of wax paper with confectioners' sugar. As soon as the cake comes out of the oven, invert it onto the wax paper. Peel off the top layer of parchment paper, place another layer of wax paper on top, then invert again. Remove the wax paper and, starting at one long end, gently roll the cake up. Wrap in a kitchen towel and cool completely at room temperature.

Make the filling:

1. Beat the whipping cream with an electric mixer until soft peaks form. Add the confectioners' sugar and vanilla extract and beat until stiff peaks form.

(Continue on next page)

Assembly:

1. Gently unroll the cake and peel off the wax paper. Spread the filling onto the surface and roll the cake back up again.

2. Wrap the cake in plastic wrap and chill in the fridge for 4 hours, or up to overnight.

3. Slice off the ends to create a clean look and place it on your work surface.

Make the frosting:

1. Beat the butter and cream cheese with an electric mixer until fluffy. Add the vanilla extract and combine.

2. Add the confectioners' sugar and beat until light and fluffy.

3. Divide the frosting into 4 bowls. Dye it pink, light blue, dark blue, and black. Place a large sheet of plastic wrap on your work surface. Dollop the buttercream onto the plastic wrap in different spots to create a marble-like pattern. Roll the plastic wrap up so that you have a long sausage of buttercream. Trim off any excess plastic wrap on each end of the sausage and place the sausage into a piping bag fitted with a large, round piping tip.

Decorate:

1. To fully coat the cake in frosting, you can elevate the cake on a couple of cups or ramekins, but this is optional.

2. Starting at one long side of the cake, pipe a row of buttercream dollops. Use a knife or an offset spatula to spread the dollops upward, creating a scallop shape. Repeat with another row of dollops right above the scallops and continue until the entire cake is covered.

3. Sprinkle some silver edible glitter on top, then gently transfer the cake to your serving plate. Enjoy!

Dragon Chow

MAKES ABOUT 5 CUPS

½ cup semisweet chocolate chips, melted
¼ cup chocolate hazelnut spread
   (e.g., Nutella)
¼ cup peanut butter
2 tablespoons unsalted butter
2½ cups corn pops cereal
2 cups honeycomb cereal
1½ cups confectioners' sugar
1 cup peanut M&M's
1 cup pretzels

1. Combine the chocolate chips, chocolate hazelnut spread, peanut butter, and unsalted butter in a bowl.

2. Pour both types of cereal into a large ziptop bag. Pour the chocolate mixture into the bag. Seal the bag and massage it with your hands until the cereal is fully coated.

3. Add the confectioners' sugar, seal the bag again, and mix until the cereal is fully coated.

4. Add the M&M's and pretzels, mix together, and serve to your dragon!

Dragon's Golden Coins

MAKES AS MANY AS NEEDED

Chocolate sandwich cookies (you can
   use full-size cookies or mini)
Edible gold color spray

1. Place the cookies on a baking sheet lined with parchment paper. Spray with the gold color spray until evenly coated.

2. Flip over and repeat on the opposite side.

3. Use these coins as your dragon's treasure when making any dragon cakes or cupcakes in this book!

Edible Embers

MAKES 4 SKEWERS' WORTH OF CANDY

2 cups water
6 cups granulated sugar
Your desired extract or flavoring
Red, orange, and yellow food coloring

4 wooden skewers
4 (6-inch) pieces of string
4 (250-milliliter) clean and empty
   mason jars with rings

Prep the skewers:
1. Wet each wooden skewer with water and then roll it in some extra granulated sugar. This creates a starting layer of sugar for the crystals to grow from.

2. Set them aside to dry.

Make the syrup:
1. Pour the water into a pot and bring to a boil. Add the sugar 1 cup at a time, mixing with each addition. Make sure the sugar is dissolved before adding another cup.

2. Once all of the sugar has been added and dissolved, remove the pan from the heat. Add a couple of drops of your desired flavoring and mix well.

3. Divide the liquid between 3 bowls. Dye one bowl red, one bowl yellow, and one bowl orange. Allow it to cool for about 30 minutes.

Grow the crystals:
1. Pour the sugar syrup into the 3 jars. Dye the remaining red syrup an even deeper shade of red and pour this into the remaining jar.

2. Tie a string around the non-sugar-coated end of each skewer so that the skewer is in the center of the string with equal amounts of string on either side.

3. Lower a skewer into each jar, keeping it about 1 inch from the bottom of the jar. Use the strings to hold the skewer in place and screw the ring of the mason jar on top, securing the strings. I also used some tape if the skewer was leaning too far in one direction.

4. Place the jars in a cool, dark place, and cover loosely with a dish towel.

5. The crystals should start growing in a couple of hours and will be fully grown in a couple of days.

6. Allow the crystals to dry for a couple of hours before using.

7. Use a sharp knife to cut the crystals off the skewers. Use them to create glowing, vibrant embers on all of your treats!

DRAGON SCALE SHEET CAKE

MAKES 1 (9 × 13-INCH) CAKE

Cake batter:
1 cup unsalted butter, room
    temperature
2 cups granulated sugar
3 teaspoons vanilla extract
6 large eggs
3 cups all-purpose flour
1 teaspoon baking soda
1 teaspoon salt
1½ cups sour cream

Buttercream:
2 cups unsalted butter, room
    temperature
1 teaspoon vanilla extract or seeds
    from 1 vanilla bean
5 cups confectioners' sugar
Red, orange, and yellow food coloring
Orange and yellow sanding sugar

Bake the cake:
1. Beat the butter and sugar with an electric mixer until pale and smooth. Add the vanilla extract and eggs one at a time, mixing with each addition.

2. In a separate bowl, combine the flour, baking soda, and salt. Add this to the batter in 2 additions, alternating with the sour cream.

3. Spoon the batter into a greased and floured 9 × 13–inch cake pan. Bake at 350°F for 1 hour 15 minutes, or until a skewer inserted into the center comes out clean. Cool completely.

Make the buttercream:
1. Beat the butter with an electric mixer until pale and fluffy. Add the vanilla extract and confectioners' sugar 1 cup at a time, beating with each addition.

Assembly:
1. Slice the top off the cake to smooth the surface and remove any excess browning.

2. Coat the top of the cake in a thin layer of buttercream, called a crumb coat. This will catch any excess cake crumbs. Chill the cake in the fridge for 20 minutes.

3. Dye two thirds of the remaining buttercream red. Of the remaining white buttercream, dye ¼ cup yellow and the remaining orange. Place both the red and orange buttercream into piping bags fitted with large, round piping tips.

4. Starting at one short side of the cake, pipe a row of buttercream dollops. Use orange dollops where you would like the spine to start. Use a knife or an offset spatula to spread the dollops upward, creating a scallop shape. Repeat with another row of dollops right above the scallops and continue until the entire cake is covered, adjusting the position of the orange dollops so that you create a wavy spine.

5. Place the yellow frosting into a piping bag fitted with a large, round piping tip. Pipe spikes down the orange spine.

6. Sprinkle orange and yellow sanding sugar down the spine.

7. Slice and enjoy!

ℰMBER DOUGHNUTS

MAKES 15-20 DOUGHNUTS

Doughnuts:
2 tablespoons active dry yeast
½ cup warm water
¼ cup + 1 teaspoon granulated sugar
2½ cups all-purpose flour
2 large eggs
Black food coloring
2 tablespoons unsalted butter, room
  temperature
2 teaspoons salt
Canola oil

Filling:
2½ cups vanilla pudding
Red and orange food coloring

Glaze:
1½ cups confectioners' sugar
½ cup whipping cream
Black food coloring

Make the doughnuts:

1. Place the yeast, warm water, and 1 teaspoon granulated sugar into the bowl of an electric mixer fitted with the dough hook attachment. Allow this to sit for 10 minutes, until the yeast develops.

2. Add the flour, ¼ cup sugar, eggs, black food coloring, butter, and salt. Set the mixer to medium speed and knead for 8 to 9 minutes, until the dough is smooth, soft, and bounces back when poked with your finger.

3. Place the dough in an oiled bowl and cover with plastic wrap. Place in a warm spot until doubled in size, about 1 hour.

4. Roll the dough out to ¼-inch-thick and cut into 2½-inch-wide circles with a cookie cutter. You should be able to get 15 to 20 doughnuts. Transfer the doughnuts to a lightly floured baking sheet and cover with a sheet of plastic wrap. Place in a warm spot and let rise for 20 minutes.

5. Pour about 5 inches of canola oil into a pot and set to medium heat. Attach a deep fry thermometer and heat the oil to 370°F. Fry 3 or 4 doughnuts at a time, cooking for 1 minute 15 seconds on each side.

6. Remove the doughnuts from the oil with a slotted spoon and place on a baking sheet lined with paper towel. Cool completely.

(Continue on page 62)

Make the filling:

1. Add 1 drop of red food coloring and several drops of orange food coloring to the vanilla pudding. This will create a glowing, vibrant orange color.

2. Place the filling in a piping bag fitted with a large, round piping tip.

Make the glaze:

1. Combine the confectioners' sugar and whipping cream in a bowl. Add a couple drops of black food coloring and mix well.

2. Set aside.

Assembly:

1. Poke a hole in the side of each doughnut with the end of a fork. Stick the end of the piping tip into the hole and fill the dough with pudding until the doughnut starts to feel heavy.

2. Dunk the doughnuts into the glaze, then allow the glaze to dry for about 15 minutes. Enjoy!

GRIFFIN CUTOUT SHEET CAKE

SERVES 8-10

Cake batter:

2 cups all-purpose flour
2 cups granulated sugar
¾ cup cocoa powder + extra for
   coating the pan
2 teaspoons baking powder
1½ teaspoons baking soda
1 teaspoon salt
1 cup milk
½ cup vegetable oil
2 large eggs
2 teaspoons vanilla extract
1 cup boiling water

Frosting:

9 ounces cream cheese, room
   temperature
1½ cups unsalted butter, room
   temperature
1 teaspoon vanilla extract
3 cups confectioners' sugar
Brown, orange, and black food
   coloring

Bake the cake:

1. Place the flour, sugar, cocoa powder, baking powder, baking soda, and salt in a large bowl and mix together.

2. Add the milk, vegetable oil, eggs, and vanilla extract and mix with an electric mixer until combined.

3. Slowly add the boiling water and mix until well combined.

4. Grease and flour a 9 × 13–inch pan.

5. Pour the batter into the pan and bake at 350°F for 50 minutes, until a skewer inserted into the center comes out clean. Cool for 15 minutes in the pan, then turn onto a wire rack and cool completely.

Make the frosting:

1. Beat the cream cheese and butter with an electric mixer until pale and fluffy.

2. Add the vanilla extract and confectioners' sugar 1 cup at a time, mixing with each addition.

Assembly:

1. Slice the top off the cake to flatten the surface and place the cake on your desired serving platter.

2. Cut 3 to 4 inches of cake off the long end of the cake and stick it to the right side of the cake. This will create the griffin's body.

3. Carve the griffin out of the cake, using scraps to create its ears. Then coat the cake in a thin, even layer.

(Continue on next page)

of frosting. The cake will be very delicate, but keep at it! This thin layer of frosting will trap the crumbs inside and prevent the crumbs from coming to the surface.

4. Divide the remaining frosting in half. Leave one half white and dye one half light brown. Place them both into piping bags fitted with small, star-shaped piping tips.

5. Pipe the griffin's head and ears with the white frosting and its body and wings with the brown frosting.

6. Dye the remaining brown frosting an even deeper shade of brown with some more brown and black food coloring. Use this frosting to outline the legs, wings, and tail.

7. Set aside a couple tablespoons of white frosting. Divide the remaining white frosting into two. Dye one bowl orange and one bowl black. Place them both into piping bags fitted with small, star-shaped piping tips.

8. Create the beak and claws with the orange frosting. And the eyes with the black and remaining white frosting.

Dragon Cake

MAKES 1 (6-INCH) CAKE

Cake batter:
1 cup unsalted butter,
  room temperature
2 cups granulated sugar
3 teaspoons vanilla extract
6 large eggs
3 cups all-purpose flour
1 teaspoon baking soda
1 teaspoon salt
1½ cups sour cream
Red and black food coloring

Buttercream:
2 cups unsalted butter,
  room temperature
1 teaspoon vanilla extract or
  seeds from 1 vanilla bean
5 cups confectioners' sugar
Black, red, blue, and orange
  food coloring

1 cup black fondant
6 lollipop sticks
Copper edible glitter
1¼ cups melted candy wafers
Gold sprinkles
1 Chocolate Dragon Snout (page 69)

Bake the cake:

1. Beat the butter and sugar with an electric mixer until pale and smooth. Add the vanilla extract and eggs one at a time, mixing with each addition.

2. In a separate bowl, combine the flour, baking soda, and salt. Add this to the batter in 2 additions, alternating with the sour cream.

3. Divide the batter into 2 bowls. Dye one bowl red and one bowl black.

4. Spoon both colors of batter into 3 greased and floured 6-inch round cake pans. Swirl with a knife to create a marble effect. Bake at 350°F for 30 to 40 minutes, or until a skewer inserted into the centers comes out clean. Cool completely.

Make the buttercream:

1. Beat the butter with an electric mixer until pale and fluffy. Add the vanilla extract and confectioners' sugar 1 cup at a time, beating with each addition.

2. Set aside ½ cup of white buttercream. Dye the remaining buttercream a reddish-orange color with the red and orange food coloring.

Make the horns:

1. Divide the black fondant into 4 pieces and roll them into 6- to 7-inch sausages.

2. Twist two together to create a spiral and pinch them together at the ends to create a horn. Curve them gently, then insert a lollipop stick into the base. Repeat with the remaining two sausages.

(Continue on page 68)

3. Place them on a sheet of plastic wrap and use a food-safe paint brush to dust the horns with copper edible glitter.

4. Allow them to harden at room temperature while you decorate the cake.

Make the wings and crown:
1. Spoon the candy wafers onto a tray lined with parchment paper, creating 2 wing shapes and a crown shape for the top of the dragon's head.

2. Stick one lollipop stick into each wing and two into the base of the crown.

3. Transfer the tray to the fridge for these to stiffen while you decorate the cake.

Assembly:
1. Slice the tops and bottoms off the cakes to smooth the surface and remove any excess browning. Keep the cake scraps!

2. Stack the cakes and spread some buttercream between each layer.

3. Coat the cake in a thin layer of buttercream, called a crumb coat. This will catch any excess cake crumbs. Chill the cake in the fridge for 20 minutes.

4. Crumble the cake scraps into a small bowl and add a couple dollops of buttercream. It should be able to be shaped into a ball and hold itself together.

5. Press this mixture onto the front of the cake to create the bridge of the dragon's snout. Use a toothpick or knife to gently etch into the cake where the dragon's eyes and snout will be.

6. Place the red buttercream into a piping bag fitted with a small- to medium-sized piping tip. Starting at the base of the cake, pipe a row of dollops. Use a chopstick or small tool (I used the tip of the handle of a small spoon) to drag the dollop upward, creating a scallop. Continue with the entire row. Pipe another

row of dollops just above the scallops and repeat until the entire cake is covered, avoiding the snout and eye area.

7. Use toothpicks to attach the Dragon Snout to the cake.

8. Stick the wings and crown to the cake and cover with a smooth layer of red buttercream.

9. Stick the horns onto the top of the cake. If you find that they are too large, you can trim some fondant off at the base of the horns.

Details and eyes:
1. Place the remaining red buttercream into a piping bag fitted with a small, star-shaped piping tip. Pipe the veins onto the wings and crown. Cover the snout with dollops of buttercream.

2. Dye about ¼ cup of the remaining red buttercream a deeper shade of red by adding some more red and orange food coloring.

3. Place it into another piping bag fitted with a small, star-shaped piping tip.

4. Pipe it on top of the veins onto the wings and crown and add some shadows onto the snout.

5. Take the reserved white buttercream and gently spread it onto the cake to create the eyes.

6. Reserve a couple tablespoons of white buttercream. Dye the reserved buttercream blue and gently spread it onto the eye to create the iris.

7. Dye the remaining blue buttercream black and create the pupil. Place the remaining black buttercream into a piping bag fitted with a small, star-shaped piping tip and pipe an outline around the eyes.

8. Sprinkle some gold sprinkles around the base of the horns. Enjoy!

CHOCOLATE DRAGON SNOUTS

MAKES 3 SNOUTS

Frosting:
⅓ cup ounces (60 grams) cream cheese, room temperature
⅓ cup unsalted butter, room temperature
1 teaspoon vanilla extract
¾ cup confectioners' sugar
Black food coloring
12 ounces (325 grams) chocolate cake (offcuts from the Dragon Cake, page 66, work great!)
2 cups milk chocolate chips, melted

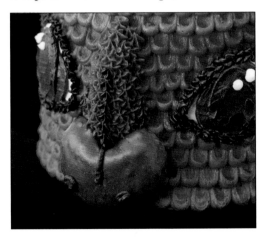

Make the frosting:
1. Place the cream cheese and butter in a bowl and beat with an electric mixer until light and fluffy. Add the vanilla extract and mix until combined.

2. Add the powdered sugar and beat for 2 to 3 minutes, until smooth.

3. Set aside about 3 tablespoons of frosting and dye it black. Place it into a piping bag fitted with a small, round piping tip.

Assemble:
1. Crumble the chocolate cake into a large bowl.

2. Add the white frosting to the bowl then mix with an electric mixer until well combined. You can use a spoon here, but the electric mixer will help break apart any larger pieces and create a smooth, cohesive dough.

3. Shape the dough into 3 snouts and place them on a baking sheet lined with parchment paper. Chill them in the fridge until stiff, about 30 minutes.

4. Working with one snout at a time, submerge a snout into the melted milk chocolate chips. Use a fork to scoop out the snout and tap the edge of the fork on the side of your bowl a couple times to encourage any excess chocolate to drip off.

5. Return the snout to the baking sheet and repeat with the remaining snouts. Then place the snouts in the fridge until the chocolate has set, about 30 to 45 minutes.

Decorate:
1. Pipe the details (the nostrils, etc.) onto the snout with the black buttercream.

2. If you are using the snouts for the Dragon Cake (page 66), I recommend attaching the snout to the cake before piping the details so that they don't get smudged.

3. Enjoy your snouts!

3D Carved Dragon Cake

MAKES 1 (15-INCH) CAKE

Cake batter:
2 cups unsalted butter,
 room temperature
4 cups granulated sugar
2 tablespoons vanilla extract
12 large eggs
6 cups all-purpose flour
2 teaspoons baking soda
2 teaspoons salt
3 cups sour cream

Buttercream:
4 cups unsalted butter,
 room temperature
3 teaspoons vanilla extract or
 seeds from 2 vanilla beans
9–10 cups confectioners' sugar

1 cup melted candy wafers
4 lollipop sticks
Purple and black food coloring
1 birthday candle with a large wick

Bake the cake:
1. Beat the butter and sugar with an electric mixer until pale and smooth. Add the vanilla extract and eggs 1 at a time, mixing with each addition.

2. In a separate bowl, combine the flour, baking soda, and salt. Add this to the batter in 2 additions, alternating with the sour cream.

3. Spoon the batter into 2 greased and floured 9 × 13–inch rectangular cake pans. Bake at 350°F for 60 to 70 minutes, or until a skewer inserted into the centers comes out clean. Cool completely.

Make the buttercream:
1. Beat the butter with an electric mixer until pale and fluffy. Add the vanilla extract and confectioners' sugar 1 cup at a time, beating with each addition.

Shape the cake:
1. Slice the tops and bottoms off the cakes to smooth the surface and remove any excess browning. Keep all cake scraps in a large bowl—you will need these!

2. Stack the cakes and spread some buttercream between each layer.

3. With one long side of the cake facing you, cut the cake in half, so you have two 9 × 6½–inch rectangles of cake. Carve one rectangle into the dragon's body, carving the curve of its waist and arch of its back into the cake. Place the cake scraps in the large scrap bowl.

(Continue on next page)

4. Trim about one third of cake off the remaining rectangle and place that one third of cake into the scrap bowl. Use the remaining cake to shape the head of the dragon.

5. Place the body and head on the platter that you will be serving the cake on and carve a little more so that the head and body fit together nicely.

6. Coat the cake in a very thin layer of frosting, then place it in the fridge to chill for about 15 minutes.

Make the wings:
1. Spoon the melted candy wafers onto a tray lined with parchment paper to create two wings. Stick two lollipop sticks onto each wing—this is how they will be attached to the cake!

2. You can use a couple layers of candy wafers to ensure that the wings will be strong enough to handle. Candy wafers harden at room temperature, so when they are about 50 percent set, you can use a sharp knife to trim and sharpen up the edges.

3. Transfer the wings to the fridge to chill while you continue to the next step.

Finish shaping the cake:
1. Use an electric mixer to crumble the large bowl of cake scraps into fine crumbs. You can use your hands to crumble the cake scraps, but an electric mixer is so much faster!

2. Add some buttercream to the cake crumbs until it can be molded like clay! Start with 1 cup of buttercream and add more as needed. It should hold its shape when rolled into a ball—not too dry and crumbly and not too soft!

3. Remove the cake from the fridge and use the cake crumbs to build the dragon's snout, ears, tail, legs, and arms. You can also use it to round out of the shape of the dragon's head and body, if desired.

4. Stick the wings into the top of the cake.

5. When shaping the tail, stick the birthday candle into the tip of the tail so that just the wick is exposed. The larger the wick, the larger the flame you will get, so keep this in mind when selecting your candle.

6. Return the cake to the fridge until the cake crumb sections have stiffened, about 20 to 30 minutes.

Decorate:
1. Coat the entire cake in a very thin, even layer of buttercream. The cool temperature of the cake should chill the buttercream as you do this and will seal any crumbs into this thin layer of frosting.

2. Set about ¼ cup of frosting aside and dye the remaining frosting purple with food coloring.

Decorate, Step 1

3. Spread an even layer of purple buttercream onto the entire cake.

4. Add some blue buttercream to the remaining purple buttercream, creating a deep, indigo color. Spread this buttercream onto the dragon's wings. Place the remaining buttercream into a piping bag fitted with a medium-sized, round piping tip. Pipe dollops down the dragon's back, tail, and ears, veins on its wings, and nostrils.

5. Place the reserved ¼ cup buttercream into a piping bag fitted with another medium-sized round piping tip. Pipe the dragon's fingernails and white eyes. Set this piping bag side.

6. Take about 3 tablespoons of remaining indigo buttercream and add a couple drops of black food coloring, dying it black. Place it in a piping bag fitted with a medium-sized round piping tip. Pipe the dragon's pupils onto the white eyes. Use the white piping bag from the previous step to add a sparkle in the dragon's eyes.

Serve:
1. To serve, light the wick at the end of the tail and enjoy!

Decorate, Step 6

Serve, Step 1

Dragon Slayer Pudding, page 104

THE MAGIC MARKET

Dragon Poison Apple

MAKES 6 APPLES

6 Granny Smith apples
Long lollipop sticks
14 ounces (400 grams) caramel
   candies
2 tablespoons milk
24 mini marshmallows
3 cups green candy wafers, melted
   + ½ cup unmelted and roughly
   chopped
4 cups green-colored sugar
12 candy eyes
¼ cup star sprinkles
12 black sprinkles
Toothpicks

1. Stick the lollipop sticks into the top of the apples; jam them right into the core. Place the apples onto a baking sheet lined with parchment paper.

2. Place the caramels and milk in a pot and set to medium heat. Keep stirring until the candies have fully melted.

3. Turn off the heat and wait for the caramel to stop bubbling. Dip each apple into the caramel sauce and fully coat it. Then place them on the baking sheet to set.

4. If any bubbles appear on the caramel, simply poke them with a sharp knife and deflate them. Stick 2 mini marshmallows onto the front of the apples to create the dragon's snout. If they

aren't attaching well, use toothpicks to help them stick to the apple.

5. Once the caramel has hardened, dip each apple into the melted green candy wafers. Allow any excess to drip off. There shouldn't be too much chocolate on each apple, just enough to act as "glue" for the sugar. Roll the apple into the green-colored sugar. You may need to roll it a couple times to get an even coating. Return the apples to the baking sheet lined with parchment paper.

6. Let the apples sit at room temperature for about 20 minutes, until the candy wafers have hardened.

7. Use some extra candy wafers to create wings on a tray lined with parchment paper. Sprinkle more green sprinkles on top and place the tray in the fridge for the wings to harden. Then attach them to the dragons with more melted candy wafers.

8. Create the horns by cutting 2 mini marshmallows into triangles. Dip the candy eyes into the green wafers to create eyelids and use black candies as the nostrils. Attach all of these to the apples with some melted candy wafers.

9. Stick the chopped candy wafers and star sprinkles to the dragon's cheeks to add some extra definition.

10. Wrap in some cellophane bags, if desired. To serve, it's easiest to slice wedges with a sharp knife instead of biting directly into the apple with your teeth!

DRAGON STEW

SERVES 4-5

Dragon dumplings:
3½ ounces (100 grams) shiratamako rice
   flour (sweet rice flour)
100 milliliters (100 grams) water
Purple and black food coloring
Ice water

Stew:
¼ small pumpkin
1 package shimeji mushrooms
1 carrot
¼ Chinese cabbage
1–2 green onions + some for garnish
¾ pound (300 grams) chicken thighs
8 cups water
2 tablespoons Japanese powdered stock
5–6 tablespoons miso paste

Make the dumplings:
1. Gradually add water to a bowl containing the shiratamako rice flour, and knead well until the dough becomes "as soft and firm as your earlobe."

2. Dye two thirds of the dough purple and half of the remaining dough black. Create 2-inch-long dumplings in the shape of dragon tails, claws, wings, teeth, etc. Use the purple for the skin and the black and white for the accents.

3. Place the dumplings in boiling water. Once they have risen to the surface, boil for 3 to 4 minutes, then drain and place in ice water to cool completely.

Make the stew:
1. Cut the pumpkin into large pieces. Separate the shimeji mushrooms from their bases, and cut the remaining vegetables and chicken thighs into bite-sized pieces.

2. Place the water, stock powder, and pumpkin into a pot, and boil for about 5 minutes. Once the pumpkin has cooked through, remove half of the pumpkin pieces, and set on a plate.

3. Add the carrot, Chinese cabbage, and mushrooms and boil for about 10 minutes. Then add and dissolve the miso paste, return the cooked pumpkin to the pot, and top with the green onion and dumplings.

4. Pour the stew into bowls to serve.

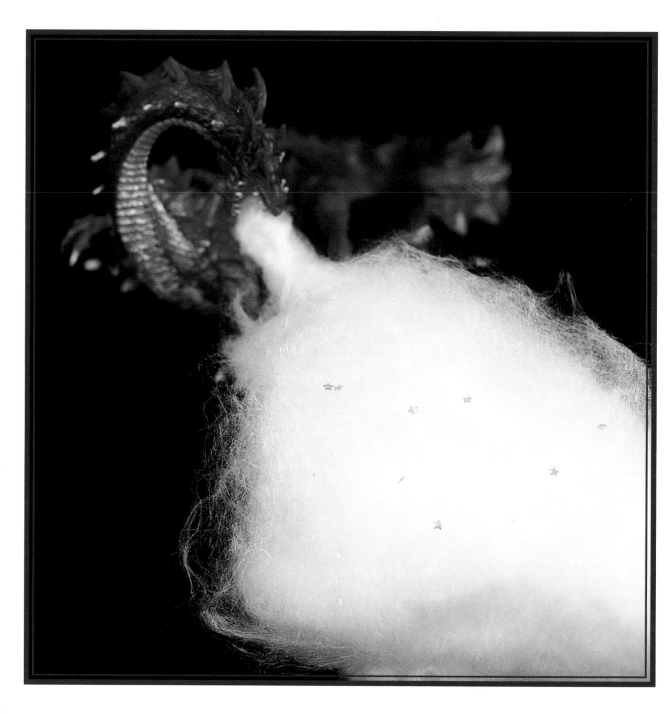

Dragon's Breath

MAKES 2 LARGE HANDFULS

1 tablespoon granulated sugar
Gold star sugar sprinkles

At-home cotton candy machine

1. Turn on your personal cotton candy machine and allow it to warm up for 2 to 3 minutes.

2. Turn off the heat and place the sugar into the center sugar bin.

3. Turn the machine back on and hold a paper straw horizontally across the top of the machine.

4. When cotton candy starts to form, rotate the straw to catch the cotton candy and spin it around the straw.

5. Once the cotton candy stops being produced, sprinkle some gold stars on it and use it in your favorite recipe!

> **For flavored dragon's breath, crush your favorite hard candies or lollipops into very, very fine pieces and use in place of sugar!**

DRAGON EYE GUMMIES

MAKES 24 (1-INCH) EYEBALLS

Iris and pupils:
2 tablespoons powdered gelatin
¼ cup + 1 tablespoon water
¾ cup orange soda
1 drop vanilla extract
Black and red food coloring

Whites of the eyes:
1 cup orange soda
½ cup powdered gelatin
1 cup condensed milk
¼ cup granulated sugar

Make the iris and pupils:
1. Combine the gelatin and water in a microwave-safe bowl. Heat for 20 to 30 seconds, until liquid.

2. Pour the orange soda, gelatin mixture, and 1 drop of vanilla extract into a small pot and set to medium heat. Heat until the gelatin has fully dissolved, then remove from the heat.

3. Use a spoon to remove any foam that has accumulated on the surface and discard. Pour ¼ cup of the gelatin mixture into a small bowl. Dye it black with a couple drops of black food coloring.

4. Use a small spoon to drop 2 to 3 drops of black jelly into each space of a 1-inch sphere ice cube mold. Use a toothpick to shape the pupils into cat-like pupils. Allow the pupils to set at room temperature while you make the iris.

5. Once the pupils are mostly set, place a dollop of the remaining orange jelly on top, creating the iris. It should extend past the ends of the pupil. Before the iris sets, dip a toothpick in red food coloring and make stripes in the orange jelly, extending out from the pupils. Allow these to set at room temperature, for about 1 hour.

Make the whites of the eyes:
1. Place the orange soda and gelatin in a microwave-safe bowl. Microwave for 20-second intervals until liquid.

2. Pour the condensed milk, sugar, and the gelatin mixture into a small pot and set it to medium heat. Mix until the gelatin has dissolved and everything is fully incorporated. Use a spoon to remove any foam that has accumulated on the surface and discard.

3. Pour the mixture into the molds and place the lid on top. Place the mold in the refrigerator overnight, or until the gummy mixture has fully set.

4. Gently unmold the eyes and enjoy!

Dragon Tail Skewers

MAKES ABOUT 1 DOZEN TAILS

⅓ cup + ¼ cup cold water
2½ teaspoons powdered gelatin
1 cup granulated sugar
Seeds from 1 vanilla bean
   (or 1 teaspoon vanilla extract)
Red and blue food coloring
¼ cup confectioners' sugar
¼ cup corn starch
Wooden skewers

1. Pour ⅓ cup of cold water into the bowl of an electric mixer and sprinkle the powdered gelatin on top. Let sit for 5 minutes.

2. Place the sugar and ¼ cup cold water in a small pot and set to medium-high heat. Stir until the sugar has melted.

3. Attach a candy thermometer to the pot and boil the sugar until it reaches 238°F. Brush the sides of the pot with a wet pastry brush if sugar crystals stick to the sides. Remove the pot from the heat and stir until the sugar stops boiling.

4. Add the hot sugar to the gelatin, and stir the mixture by hand, whisking for a few minutes to slightly cool. Then beat with an electric mixer on medium-high speed for 8 to 10 minutes, until soft peaks form. Add the vanilla bean seeds or extract and mix until combined. Add a couple drops of red food coloring and mix well.

5. Place the marshmallow mixture in a piping bag fitted with a large, round piping tip. Line a baking sheet with parchment paper and pipe long tails onto the paper.

6. Add some blue food coloring to the remaining marshmallow to dye it purple. Return it to a piping bag fitted with a large, round piping tip, and pipe spikes along the tails.

7. Allow the marshmallow to stiffen at room temperature for 6 hours, or overnight, until firm to the touch.

8. Combine the confectioners' sugar and corn starch in a bowl and place in a mesh sieve. Dust over the surface of the marshmallow. Unstick the marshmallows from the pan with a butter knife and dust the underside of the marshmallows with the sugar coating.

9. Bounce in a mesh sieve to remove any excess coating, and stick onto wooden skewers! These are best consumed within 24 hours.

Dragon Blood

SERVES 2

½ cup pink dragon fruit
½ cup frozen strawberries, thawed
1 cup fresh lemon juice
2 tablespoons sugar syrup, honey, or
   corn syrup
1–2 cups sparkling water

1. Place the dragon fruit and frozen strawberries in a blender and pulse until smooth.

2. Strain through a cheesecloth or fine mesh sieve to remove any seeds and pulp. You just want the juice!

3. Mix the juice with the lemon juice, sugar syrup, and sparkling water.

4. Pour over ice to serve!

Dragon Blood Punch

SERVES 2

⅓ cup grenadine
1¼ cups blue Kool-Aid
1 cup lemon-lime soda (e.g., Sprite)
6–8 Dragon Eye Gummies (page 82)

1. Combine the grenadine, Kool-Aid, and soda in a bowl.

2. Divide between two glasses.

3. Slide some Dragon Eye Gummies onto two skewers, and drop a couple extra into the bottom of both glasses. Enjoy!

DRAGON EYE BOBA

MAKES ABOUT ²/₃ CUP BOBA

3½ ounces (100 grams) silken tofu
3½ ounces (100 grams) tapioca starch
Red, orange, and black edible ink pens

1. Combine the tofu and tapioca starch in a bowl and mix together until they form a cohesive dough.

2. Roll the dough into tiny balls. Have a bubble tea straw with you to ensure you're making boba that will fit in your straw! Set the boba on a plate lined with plastic wrap, as it will stick to plastic or ceramic plates.

3. Use edible ink pens to draw the color on the irises and pupils.

4. Drop the boba into a pot of boiling water. Once they float to the surface, boil for about 5 minutes.

5. Drain and place in a bowl filled with ice water to stop the cooking.

6. Serve with your favorite tea, smoothie, or juice! Clear liquids will allow you to see the eyes more clearly.

DRAGON SLIME

SERVES 3-4

2 cups melted white chocolate
10 ounces cream cheese
1 cup whipping cream
1 batch lemon curd from Dragon Lemon
   Meringue Pie (page 132)
Purple food coloring

Egg molds

Make the eggshells:

1. Spread the white chocolate onto the inside of 8 egg half molds. The eggs should be about 4 inches tall. Place the mold in the freezer for the chocolate to set, about 30 minutes.

2. Once the chocolate has set, unmold the egg halves. Fill a bowl with boiling water and place a plate on top. The hot water will heat the plate. Place the eggs edge-side down onto the warm plate. This will melt the edges and create smooth, flat edges.

3. Return the eggshells to the fridge while you make the slime.

Make the slime:

1. Place the cream cheese in a large bowl and beat with an electric mixer until light and fluffy. Add the whipping cream and beat until stiff peaks form.

2. Add a couple drops of purple food coloring to the lemon curd to dye it a vibrant purple color. Add it to the whipped cream mixture and gently fold until fully combined.

Assembly:

1. Fill one half of the eggshells with the slime. Return the other half of the shells to the warm plate (you may need to boil the water again) and melt the edges of the eggshells.

2. While the edges are still wet, place the eggshell on top of an egg filled with slime. The melted edges will act as glue and seal the egg closed.

3. To eat, crack the egg open with a spoon and enjoy!

CRACKLED DRAGON EGGS

MAKES 8 EGGS

8 large eggs
Ice water
1½ cups soy sauce
2 cups water
2 slices fresh ginger
½ teaspoon ground cinnamon
½ teaspoon ground anise (or 1 whole star anise)
Large pinch of black pepper

1. Place the whole eggs in a pot of water. Bring to a boil, then remove from the heat, place a lid on the pot and leave the eggs for 5 minutes. This will create soft-boiled eggs.

2. Remove the eggs from the hot water and place in a bowl of ice water. This will stop the cooking.

3. Tap the eggs gently on your counter to create cracks all over the shell. **Do not peel them yet!**

4. Place the eggs in a small pot. Add the soy sauce, water, ginger, cinnamon, anise, and black pepper. The eggs should be covered completely.

5. Bring to a boil, then reduce to a simmer, and cook for 25 to 30 minutes. Remove from the heat and allow the eggs to steep in the liquid for an additional 30 minutes. Then remove the eggs and allow them to cool.

6. Peel and enjoy!

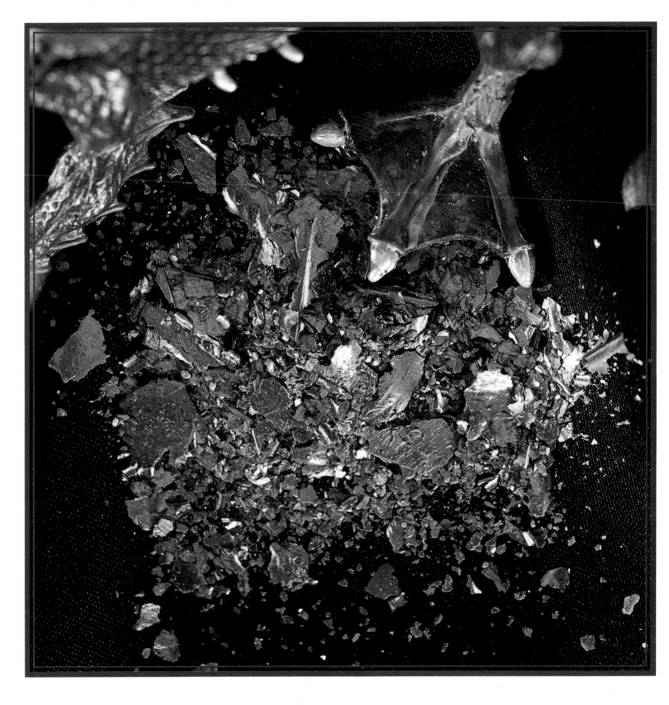

DRAGON SCALE DUST

MAKES ¼ CUP

5 teaspoons gelatin powder
¼ cup water
1 teaspoon pearl dust in your desired color

1. Pour the water into a bowl and sprinkle the gelatin on top. Allow the gelatin to develop for 5 minutes.

2. Microwave for 30 seconds, or until melted. Remove any foam.

3. Add the pearl dust and mix until fully incorporated.

4. Line the back of a large baking sheet with plastic wrap. Use a pastry brush to brush the gelatin mixture onto the plastic wrap. Try to keep the layer thin and even.

5. Allow the gelatin to dry until hard and crispy, about 12 hours or overnight.

6. Peel it off the plastic wrap and break it into pieces. Place it in a food processor or coffee grinder and pulse until it is ground as fine as you'd like.

7. Use in whatever recipes you'd like as a topping or decoration! Sprinkle on Dragon Cake (page 66), on top of the Dragon Tear Drops (page 19), as an alternative coating for one of the Dragon Egg Cheese Balls (page 21), or onto the dragon's spine for the 3D Carved Dragon Cake (page 71) or Sea Dragon Bundt Cake (page 109).

Dragon Eye Cupcakes

MAKES 10 CUPCAKES

Cupcakes:
1 cup all-purpose flour
1 cup granulated sugar
⅓ cup cocoa powder
1 teaspoon baking powder
¾ teaspoon baking soda
½ teaspoon salt
½ cup milk
¼ cup vegetable oil
1 large egg
1 teaspoon vanilla extract
½ cup boiling water

Eyeballs:
4 cups lemon-lime soda (e.g., Sprite)
3 tablespoons gelatin
2 tablespoons granulated sugar

Ganache:
1½ cups white chocolate, melted
⅓ cup whipping cream, hot
Red, orange, and yellow food coloring

Pupils:
2 ounces semisweet chocolate
2 tablespoons whipping cream, hot

Chocolate buttercream:
1 cup unsalted butter, room temperature
1 tablespoon vanilla extract
¼ cup milk
2 cups confectioners' sugar
¾ cup cocoa powder

Bake the cupcakes:

1. Place the flour, sugar, cocoa powder, baking powder, baking soda, and salt in a large bowl and mix together.

2. Add the milk, vegetable oil, egg, and vanilla extract and mix with an electric mixer until combined.

3. Slowly add the boiling water and mix until well combined.

4. Pour the batter into a lined cupcake pan (you will get 10 cupcakes), and bake at 350°F for 15 to 20 minutes, until a skewer inserted into the centers comes out clean. Cool for 15 minutes in the pan, then turn onto a wire rack and cool completely.

Make the eyeballs:

1. Pour the soda into a pot and sprinkle the gelatin on top. Allow the gelatin to develop for about 5 minutes.

2. Set the pot to medium heat and whisk until the gelatin has melted. Add the sugar and whisk until dissolved.

3. Place a half sphere mold onto a baking sheet. The spheres should be about 2 inches in diameter—almost as wide as the top of a cupcake. Pour the jelly into 10 cavities and place them in the fridge until set, about 1 to 2 hours.

(Continue on next page)

Make the white chocolate ganache:
1. Combine the melted white chocolate and hot whipping cream in a bowl. Mix until it is smooth and silky.

2. Add a couple drops of food coloring to dye it yellow.

Assembly:
1. Slice off the tops of the cupcakes to create a flat surface. Spread the ganache onto the top of the cupcake.

2. Dip a toothpick in some red and orange food coloring and paint it onto the yellow ganache. This will create the iris.

Make the pupils:
1. Finely chop the semisweet chocolate. Pour the hot whipping cream on top and allow to sit for 3 to 4 minutes. Stir until the chocolate has melted and is fully combined with the cream.

2. Use a small spoon to dollop some ganache onto the cupcake and spread it upward and downward to create a pupil. Try to keep the pupil as flat as possible, so that the jelly will sit flat.

3. Place the cupcakes in the fridge while you make the frosting.

Make the buttercream:
1. Beat the butter with an electric mixer until pale and fluffy. Add the vanilla extract and milk and mix well. Add the confectioners' sugar and cocoa powder 1 cup at a time, beating with each addition.

2. Place it into a piping bag fitted with a medium-sized, star-shaped piping tip.

Finish the cupcakes:
1. Gently unmold the jellies and place one on top of each cupcake. If you're having trouble unmolding them, dip the bottom of the mold in hot water.

2. Pipe a ring of buttercream around the edge of the jelly so that it keeps it in place.

3. Serve and enjoy!

DRAGON EXTRACT

SERVES 2-3

2 cups sparkling water
1⅓ cups pineapple juice
½ cup grapefruit juice
¼ cup lime juice
Gold edible glitter

1. Combine all liquids in a jug. Add 2 to 3 teaspoons of gold edible glitter, and stir until well combined.

2. Pour the juice into little jars and decorate with a Dragon Extract label. Instruct your guests to swirl the juice to see the gold sparkle effect!

Dragon Crest Cookie Cake

MAKES 1 (12-INCH) COOKIE CAKE

1 cup unsalted butter, room
    temperature
½ cup granulated sugar
1 cup brown sugar
1 teaspoon salt
2 teaspoons vanilla extract
2 large eggs
2¼ cups all-purpose flour
½ teaspoon baking soda
2 cups chocolate chips
Cooking spray
Edible ink pen (optional)
1 batch frosting from Dragon Scale
    Roll Cake, white (page 53)
Yellow and red food coloring

Step 5

1. Beat the butter, granulated sugar, and brown sugar in a bowl with an electric mixer until smooth. Add the salt, vanilla, and eggs and mix well. Add the flour and baking soda and mix until combined. Add the chocolate chips and mix until evenly incorporated.

2. Spray a 12-inch heart-shaped cookie pan with cooking spray. Use a rubber spatula to press the cookie dough into the pan. Bake at 350°F for 15 to 20 minutes, until the edges are golden. Cool in the pan completely.

3. Use a serrated knife to trim off the two rounded edges at the top of the heart, creating a crest shape. Use an edible ink pen to sketch the outline of the dragon onto the cookie.

4. Dye the frosting yellow and place it in a piping bag fitted with a small, star-shaped piping tip.

5. Pipe a border around dragon sketch and cover the rest of the cookie in dollops of yellow frosting.

6. Return the frosting to the bowl and add some red food coloring to dye it an orangey red. Place it in a piping bag fitted with a small, star-shaped piping tip.

7. Pipe a border around the crest and fill in the dragon sketch with the red frosting.

8. Slice and enjoy!

Amber-Trapped Dragons

MAKES 2 DOZEN (1-INCH) CANDIES

2½ cups granulated sugar
1 cup water
1½ cups light corn syrup
1 ounce dark chocolate, melted

Step 2

Make the amber:

1. Set a pot over medium heat and add the granulated sugar, water, and light corn syrup. Stir with a rubber spatula until everything is melted and combined. Then increase the heat to medium-high and attach a candy thermometer to the pot. Heat the sugar until it reaches 310°F. Keep heating until it becomes a deep amber color.

2. Remove the pot from the heat and stir until it stops bubbling.

3. Use a ladle to pour the candy into small half sphere molds. If using a silicone mold, you can pour the candy right in. If using a hard plastic mold, be sure to spray the mold with cooking spray first. This will prevent the candy from sticking.

4. Leave the amber at room temperature for 2 to 3 hours, until fully cooled and hardened. Then unmold and set aside.

Decorate:

1. Use a toothpick or small brush to paint little dragons on the flat sides of the amber.

2. You can draw whole dragons or parts of dragons, as many things can get trapped in amber!

Dragon Slayer Pudding

MAKES 2-3 PUDDINGS

Pudding:
¾ cup sugar
½ cup cocoa powder
¼ cup corn starch
3 cups milk
1 teaspoon vanilla extract
Crushed chocolate sandwich cookies
   (e.g., Oreos)

Skulls:
1 cup melted white chocolate
¼ cup chocolate hazelnut spread
   (e.g., Nutella)
10 fresh raspberries
Cocoa powder
¼ cup royal icing (from Dragon
   Sugar Cookies, page 22)

3D skull mold

Make the pudding:
1. Place the sugar, cocoa powder, and corn starch in a pot and mix to combine. Gradually add the milk, stirring to combine.

2. Set to low heat and bring to a boil. Boil for 2 minutes, stirring constantly, until thickened.

3. Remove from the heat, pour into a bowl, add the vanilla extract, and stir to combine.

4. Cover the surface with a sheet of plastic wrap and place in the fridge until chilled.

Make the skulls:
1. Spread a layer of white chocolate onto the inside of a 10-cavity 3D skull mold. The skulls should be about 1-inch high. Place the mold in the freezer for the chocolate to set, about 15 minutes.

2. Place a dollop of chocolate hazelnut spread into each cavity and place a raspberry on top.

3. Pour more white chocolate on top, then place the lid on the mold and place it in the freezer to set, about 1 hour.

4. Once the skulls have set, unmold them, and brush some cocoa powder onto them with a food-safe paint brush. This will add definition to the skulls and allow you to see all the details.

Skulls, Step 1

Skulls, Step 2

Make the bones:

1. Fill a mini bone mold with the royal icing. Allow the royal icing to dry at room temperature, about 1 to 2 hours.

Assemble:

1. Divide the pudding between bowls. Top with some crushed chocolate sandwich cookies.

2. Place a couple skulls into each bowl and nestle a couple bones around the skulls. Enjoy!

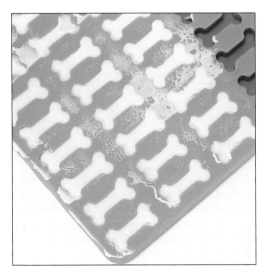

Bones, Step 1

Sea Eggs, page 114

UNDER THE SEA

Sea Dragon Bundt Cake

SERVES 10-12

Cake batter:

1 cup unsalted butter,
  room temperature
2 cups granulated sugar
3 teaspoons vanilla extract
6 large eggs
3 cups all-purpose flour
1 teaspoon baking soda
1 teaspoon salt
1½ cups sour cream
Blue food coloring
1 cup confetti sprinkles

Buttercream:

3 cups unsalted butter,
  room temperature
1½ teaspoons vanilla extract or
  seeds from 1 vanilla bean
7½ cups confectioners' sugar
Blue, green, yellow, and black food
  coloring

2 white candy wafers

Bake the cake:

1. Beat the butter and sugar with an electric mixer until pale and smooth. Add the vanilla extract and eggs one at a time, mixing with each addition.

2. In a separate bowl, combine the flour, baking soda, and salt. Add this to the batter in 2 additions, alternating with the sour cream. Dye the batter blue with the blue food coloring. Add the confetti sprinkles and gently fold to combine.

3. Spoon the batter into a greased and floured bundt pan. Bake at 350°F for 1 hour 20 minutes, or until a skewer inserted into the center comes out clean. Cool completely.

Make the buttercream:

1. Beat the butter with an electric mixer until pale and fluffy. Add the vanilla extract and confectioners' sugar one cup at a time, beating with each addition.

Assembly:

1. Slice the bottom off the cake to smooth the surface and create a flat base. Save the scraps in a bowl.

2. Cut the cake in half, so you have two C-shaped cakes. Arrange them on your serving platter to create a wiggling serpent. Coat the cake in a thin layer of buttercream, called a crumb coat. This will catch any excess cake crumbs. Chill.

(Continue on next page)

3. Crumble the scraps into a large bowl and add 1 to 2 cups of buttercream, until you create a cake pop texture! This means that the cake crumbs should hold their shape when rolled into a ball.

4. Use the cake pop mixture to create the snout, horns, fins, and tail. You may need to carve the actual cake a little bit to ensure it blends seamlessly with the added parts. Make sure the forehead slopes downward into the snout and the tail gradually gets smaller. Place the cake in the fridge for 20 minutes for the attachments to stiffen.

To decorate:

1. Divide the remaining buttercream in half. Dye one half yellow and one half light blue.

2. Place the yellow into a piping bag fitted with a small, star-shaped piping tip.

3. Start at the belly of the serpent and pipe about 3 rows of dollops. On the fourth row, leave some space between each dollop. This will help it visually blend into the next color. Pipe some yellow onto the horns as well.

4. Return the yellow buttercream to the bowl and add a drop or two of blue food coloring to create a vibrant green color. Return the buttercream to the piping bag and pipe another 2 or 3 rows of green dollops above the yellow. On the last row, be sure to leave some gaps again for the next color.

5. Set the remaining green buttercream aside for now and switch to the light blue buttercream. Place it into a piping bag fitted with a small, star-shaped piping tip. Pipe about 4 to 5 rows onto the serpent, leaving some space in the top row. Also pipe the majority of the face with the light blue buttercream.

6. Return the light blue buttercream to the bowl, and add some more blue food coloring to create a royal blue color. Place it in the piping bag and pipe enough rows to reach the sides of the fins. Again, leave some space for the next color in the final row.

7. Combine both the remaining green buttercream and blue buttercream together, then add a couple drops of black food coloring, to create a deep teal color. Return this to the piping bag and fill in any missing spots. I also used this color for the nostrils.

8. Finally, stick the white candy wafers onto the cake as the dragon's eyes. Dye a couple remaining tablespoons of buttercream black and use this for the pupils and eyelids.

Loch Ness Monster Trifle

FILLS 1 (3.25-QUART) TRIFLE DISH

Matcha cake:
1 cup unsalted butter,
   room temperature
2 cups granulated sugar
3 teaspoons vanilla extract
6 large eggs
3 cups all-purpose flour
3 tablespoons matcha green tea
   powder
1 teaspoon baking soda
1 teaspoon salt
1½ cups sour cream
Cooking spray

Coconut pudding:
1 cup granulated sugar
6 tablespoons cornstarch
Pinch salt
4 large egg yolks
1 cup heavy cream
3 cups coconut cream
1 teaspoon vanilla extract
1 teaspoon coconut extract
¼ cup unsalted butter

1¼ Matcha Dragon Doughnuts
   (page 14)
4 unmelted candy wafers

(Ingredients continue on next page)

Bake the cake:
1. Beat the butter and sugar with an electric mixer until pale and smooth. Add the vanilla extract, and eggs one at a time, mixing with each addition.

2. In a separate bowl, combine the flour, matcha green tea powder, baking soda, and salt. Add this to the batter in 2 additions, alternating with the sour cream.

3. Spoon the batter into a greased and floured bundt pan. Bake at 350°F for 45 to 60 minutes, or until a skewer inserted into the cake comes out clean. Cool completely.

Make the pudding:
1. Pour the sugar, cornstarch, and salt into a pot. Whisk to combine. Add the egg yolks and heavy cream and whisk until well combined. Add the coconut cream and mix well.

2. Set the pot to medium-high heat and whisk constantly for 5 to 10 minutes, until the mixture has thickened and is bubbling.

3. Pour the pudding through a sieve, then add the vanilla extract, coconut extract, and butter, whisking until well combined.

4. Press a sheet of plastic wrap onto the surface of the pudding and place in the fridge until chilled, about 3 hours.

Create the monster:
1. Cut the unmelted candy wafers in half and stick them into the edges of the doughnuts to look like fins. Stick 3 onto each side of the whole doughnut and 2 onto the smaller piece of doughnut.

(Continue on next page)

1½ cups melted light green candy
wafers
¼ cup melted dark green candy
wafers

1 carton strawberries
1 (8-ounce) tub whipped topping
(e.g., Cool Whip), thawed
2 teaspoons matcha green tea powder

2. Dunk the doughnuts into the melted light green candy wafers and coat completely.

3. Allow the excess to drizzle off, then place them on a tray lined with parchment paper. While the candy wafers are still wet, cut the whole doughnut in half with a sharp knife.

4. Add spots to the doughnuts with the melted darker green candy wafers.

5. Place the doughnuts into the fridge for the candy wafers to set.

Assemble:
1. Cut the bundt cake into slices and arrange them at the bottom of a trifle dish.

2. Spoon the coconut pudding on top and between the cake slices.

3. Hull and cut the strawberries in half. Place the prettiest ones along the outer edge of the trifle, then fill in the middle with the rest of the strawberries.

4. Spoon the whipped topping on top and create a wavy, swirly pattern on the surface.

5. Dust the surface with matcha green tea powder, then top with your monster!

Sea Eggs

MAKES 4-5 EGGS

Baby dragons:
½ cup cold water
¼ cup powdered gelatin
½ cup sweetened condensed milk
2 tablespoons granulated sugar
Blue and black food coloring

Eggs:
2 cups lemon-lime soda (e.g., Sprite)
2 tablespoons gelatin
2 tablespoons sugar

Dragon mold
Egg mold

Make the baby dragons:
1. Pour the cold water into a pot and add the gelatin. Allow the gelatin to develop for 5 minutes.

2. Set the pot to medium heat and whisk constantly until the gelatin has melted and is liquid.

3. Add the sweetened condensed milk and sugar and whisk until fully combined. Remove it from the heat.

4. Place your dragon molds onto a tray that will fit in your fridge. Dye a couple tablespoons of jelly a medium blue color with blue food coloring, another tablespoon dark blue, and another tablespoon black. Use a small spoon, brush, or toothpick to color in the features of the mold with these colors of jelly. These will set at room temperature because they are such small quantities of jelly.

5. Dye the remaining large amount of jelly a very pale blue and fill the molds the remainder of the way. Place the molds in the fridge until fully set, about 1 to 2 hours.

Make the eggs:
1. Once the baby dragons have been made and successfully unmolded, it's time to make the eggs!

2. Pour the soda into a pot and sprinkle gelatin on top. Allow it to bloom for about 5 minutes.

3. Set the pot to medium heat and whisk until the gelatin has fully dissolved. Add the sugar and whisk until dissolved.

4. Place a half egg mold onto a tray that will fit into your fridge. Also ensure that the baby dragons will fit into your egg mold!

5. Fill four eggs completely with jelly and place the eggs in the fridge until set, about 1 hour. The baby dragons can also be returned to the fridge during this period.

6. Once the four eggs have set, gently unmold them. You may need to place the mold in a pan of hot water to help unmold them.

7. Unmold the eggs and set them aside on a plate, flat side down. Pour the remaining jelly into four more egg molds. If the jelly is still liquid, place the molds in the fridge until the jelly is about 30% set. If it has also started to slightly set, you can skip the fridge step.

8. Place the baby dragons into the semi-set jelly, facing downward. This is so they will be facing out of the egg once you unmold it! Press the baby dragons deep enough into the jelly so that they are fully submerged.

9. Place one set egg half directly on top of the semi-set egg and voila—you have a 3D egg!

10. Return the mold to the fridge for the jelly to fully set, about 1 hour just to be safe.

11. Serve with whipped cream, whipped topping, or fresh fruit.

Dragon Egg Punch

SERVES 6

6 teaspoons butterfly pea flower tea
6 cups boiling water

Lemonade:
1½ cups granulated sugar
1 cup water
2 cups freshly squeezed lemon juice
5 cups sparkling water

3D egg mold

Serve, Step 2

Make the eggs:
1. Place the loose butterfly pea flower tea into a tea bag and steep it in 6 cups of boiling water for about 5 minutes, until the water is very blue. Cool to room temperature.

2. Place six 3D egg molds onto a tray that will easily fit in your freezer. Pour the tea into the molds and freeze until frozen solid, about 6 hours or overnight.

Make the lemonade:
1. Bring the sugar and 1 cup water to boil in a pot over medium heat. Stir until the sugar has completely dissolved, then allow to fully cool. Popping this into the freezer for 10 minutes or so will speed up the process!

2. Add the lemon juice and sparkling water.

To serve:
1. Place an egg in your glass. This effect will work best if the egg has been out of the freezer for about 10 minutes and is just starting to melt on the edges.

2. Pour the lemonade into the glass and watch as the lemonade turns purple!

Blue Dragon Cakesicles

MAKES 6 CAKESICLES

2 cups melted blue candy wafers
17 ounces (500 grams) chocolate cake
   (Griffin sheet cake, page 63)
1 cup cream cheese frosting (Griffin sheet
   cake, page 63)
2 cups white modeling chocolate
Orange, blue, and black food coloring
Blue edible glitter
Lemon extract

Cakesicle mold
6 popsicle sticks

1. Spread the melted candy wafers onto the inside of 6 cavities of a cakesicle mold. Stick the popsicle sticks into the mold, then place the mold in the fridge until the candy wafers have hardened, about 15 minutes.

2. Crumble the chocolate cake into a large bowl. Add the cream cheese frosting and mix until well combined.

3. Fill the cakesicle mold with the chocolate cake mix, then top with more melted candy wafers, sealing the cake inside. Return the cakesicle mold to the fridge while you make the decorations.

4. Dye three quarters of the modeling chocolate orange with some food coloring. Dye half of the remaining modeling chocolate blue, and leave the remaining white.

5. Shape the orange modeling chocolate into the dragon's tail, creating 3 separate segments to make it appear as if it is wrapping around the cakesicle. Create the eye by wrapping some orange modeling chocolate around a ball of white modeling chocolate and pinching it at the sides. Blot some extra blue and black food coloring directly onto the eye to create the iris and pupil. Create the claws by making three orange sausages, then pinch them to create knuckles. Use a sharp knife to create creases on each knuckle, then some extra white modeling chocolate for the nails.

6. Once the cakesicles have set, remove them from the mold. In a small dish, combine the blue edible glitter with a couple drops of lemon extract, until it resembles paint. Use a piece of paper towel to blot the edible glitter onto the cakesicles.

7. Stick the decorations onto the cakesicles and enjoy!

Sea Dragon Nest

MAKES 2 NESTS

1½ cups lemon-lime soda (e.g., Sprite)
3 tablespoons gelatin
3 tablespoons granulated sugar
½ cup brewed butterfly pea flower tea
1 teaspoon lemon juice
Purple and blue food coloring
Cooking spray
6 blackberries
Silver food coloring spray
Gold star sugar sprinkles

1. Pour the soda into a pot and sprinkle the gelatin on top. Allow it to bloom for about 5 minutes.

2. Set the pot to medium heat and whisk until it has melted. Add the sugar and mix well.

3. Divide the jelly into 3 bowls. Add ¼ cup butterfly pea flower tea to one bowl and 2 tablespoons each to the other bowls. Add lemon juice to one of the bowls with 2 tablespoons of tea.

4. If desired, add some food coloring to brighten the jelly. Add 1 to 2 drops of blue food coloring to the bowl with the most butterfly pea flower tea. Add 1 to 2 drops of purple food coloring to the bowl with the lemon juice and leave the remaining bowl clear.

5. Grease 3 (6 × 6–inch) square pans with cooking spray. Pour the jelly into the pans and place in the fridge until set, about 1 hour.

6. Unmold the jelly and slice them into thin strips.

7. Place the blackberries on a square of paper towel and spray with the silver food coloring spray to look like bumpy dragon eggs.

8. To serve, swirl the jelly noodles onto a plate and place the berries in the middle. Sprinkle some gold star sprinkles on top and enjoy!

Icy Dragon Horns

MAKES 6 HORNS

¾ cup granulated sugar
½ cup water
1 cup freshly squeezed lemon juice
2½ cups water
Blue food coloring
¼ cup frozen blueberries

1. Bring the sugar and ½ cup water to boil in a pot over medium heat. Stir until the sugar has completely dissolved, then allow to fully cool. Popping this into the freezer for 10 minutes or so will speed up the process!

2. Add the lemon juice and remaining 2½ cups water. Add only 1 drop of blue food coloring—you want it to be VERY pale blue!

3. Pour the juice into a cone-shaped popsicle mold. Leave about 1 inch of space at the top. Reserve any leftover juice.

4. Freeze the popsicles for 1 hour or until semi-frozen. Remove the popsicles from the freezer and fill the rest of the well with frozen blueberries and some remaining juice. Replace the popsicle sticks, return the mold to the freezer, and freeze until the popsicles are frozen solid, 6 hours or up to overnight.

5. When ready to serve, remove the popsicles and use a food-safe paintbrush to paint a little bit of blue food coloring directly onto the popsicles. This will create the pretty ombre effect!

6. Return the popsicles to the mold and freeze for another 15 minutes or so, then serve!

Dragon Fruit Tart, page 135

Up In The Clouds

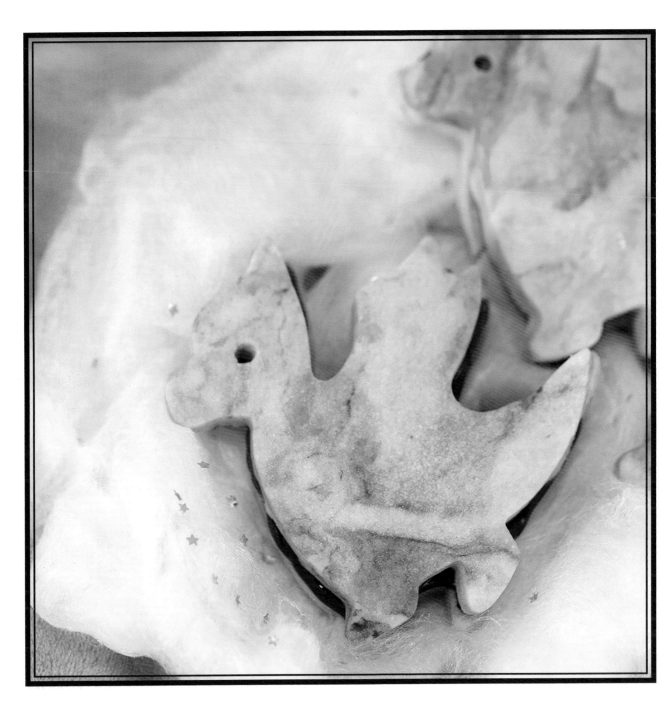

Dragon Shortbread Sandwich Cookies

MAKES 8 SANDWICH COOKIES

2 cups unsalted butter, room temperature
1 cup confectioners' sugar
2 teaspoons vanilla extract
4 cups all-purpose flour
1½ teaspoons salt
Blue food coloring
1½ cups chocolate hazelnut spread
   (e.g., Nutella)

Dragon-shaped cookie cutter

1. Preheat the oven to 325°F. Beat the butter with an electric mixer until pale and fluffy. Add the confectioners' sugar and beat for 2 minutes, until well combined. Add the vanilla and combine. In a separate bowl, combine the flour and salt, then add to the butter mixture. Mix until the dough sticks together when pinched. Add a couple drops of blue food coloring onto the dough and knead just a couple times until the dough looks marbled.

2. Wrap the dough in plastic wrap and refrigerate until firm, about 1 hour.

3. Roll the dough out on a floured surface to ¼ inch thick. Use a dragon-shaped cookie cutter to cut out 16 cookies. Place them on a baking sheet lined with parchment paper.

4. Use a chopstick or skewer to poke eye holes in half of the dragons.

5. Refrigerate the cookies until firm, about 30 minutes.

6. Bake at 325°F for 13 to 15 minutes. Cool on the pan for 10 minutes, then transfer to a wire rack and cool completely.

7. Spread Nutella onto the cookies without the eye holes and place a cookie with an eye hole on top. Enjoy!

DRAGON WING STAINED GLASS COOKIES

MAKES ABOUT 18 (3-INCH) COOKIES

1 batch Sugar Cookie dough (from Dragon
   Sugar Cookies, page 22)
1 cup lightly crushed hard candies

1. Preheat the oven to 350°F.

2. Roll the dough out on a floured surface to about
¼-inch thick. Use a cookie cutter or your own stencil to
cut out dragon wings.

3. Place the wings on a baking sheet lined with
parchment paper. Cut out windows in the wings and
place hard candies in their place.

4. Bake the cookies for about 10 minutes, until the
edges of the cookies begin to brown and the candies
have melted and filled the windows.

5. Allow the cookies to cool completely on the baking
sheet. Then enjoy!

Dragon Palace Charcuterie Board

SERVES 4-5

1 carton strawberries
5 cubes white cheese
1 Dragon Egg Cheese Ball with crackers
(page 21)
⅓ cup hummus
Dragon Scale Dust (optional, page 95)
Fresh cucumbers
Fresh carrots
Fresh radishes
2 Dragon Meringue Pops (page 145)
3 Dragon Claw Truffles (page 50)
Dragon Chow (page 55)

Strawberry dragon tail:

1. Slice the strawberries in half, then arrange on your plate to look like a scaly tail.

2. Cut the cheese into triangles and place them onto the tail as spikes.

3. Nestle the Dragon Egg Cheese Ball and crackers into the curve of the tail.

Crudite:

1. Place the hummus in a small ramekin and sprinkle some Dragon Scales on top.

2. Place on the cheese board, along with some fresh carrots, cucumbers, and radish.

To finish:

1. Add a sweet touch to the board with some Dragon Chow, Dragon Claw Truffles, and Dragon Meringue Pops.

Dragon Lemon Meringue Pie

MAKES 1 (9-INCH) TART

Lemon curd:

8 large eggs

2¼ cups granulated sugar

1¼ cups fresh lemon juice
(about 8 lemons)

½ cup + 2 tablespoons unsalted
butter, cold and cut into cubes

Zest from 5 lemons

Crust:

6½ ounces (180 grams) graham
crackers

5 tablespoons unsalted butter, melted

Meringue:

4 egg whites, room temperature

1 cup granulated sugar

¼ teaspoon vanilla extract

2 candy eyes

Make the curd:

1. Place a pot over medium heat and add the eggs, sugar, and lemon juice. Whisk until blended, then add the butter and lemon zest.

2. Cook, whisking constantly, until the mixture has thickened and coats the back of a spoon.

3. Transfer to a bowl and cool for 10 minutes. Then cover with plastic wrap and chill in the refrigerator until cold.

Make the crust:

1. Crumble the graham crackers by pulsing them in a food processor or crushing them in a ziptop bag.

2. Mix them with the melted butter until fully incorporated and they feel like damp sand.

3. Press the mixture into a 9-inch round tart pan with a removable bottom. Press the sides in first, then press the remaining mixture into the bottom of the pan.

4. Place the tart crust into the fridge to chill, for about 30 minutes.

5. Fill the crust with the lemon curd, smooth the surface, and return to the fridge while you make the meringue.

Make the meringue:

1. In a large bowl, beat the egg whites with an electric mixer until frothy. Slowly add the sugar while continuing to mix at medium-high speed. Keep beating until the

(Continue on page 134)

meringue is no longer gritty when rubbed between your fingers and holds stiff peaks. Then add the vanilla extract and mix until combined.

2. Spoon the meringue into a piping bag fitted with a large, round piping tip.

3. Remove the tart from the fridge and pipe the dragon's head, body, and snout. Don't be shy when piping—you need to pipe with force to build up the height of the body with the meringue.

4. Switch the piping tip to a medium round piping tip and pipe the dragon's tail, arms, and spikes. Switch to a small piping tip and pipe the dragon's fingers and toes, nostrils, ears, horns, and spots on its body. You can also pipe little dollops on the rest of the surface of the pie.

5. Use a kitchen blow torch to gently brown the dragon. Then stick the candy eyes to the dragon's face.

6. Slice and enjoy!

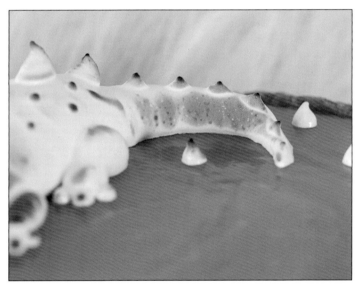

Step 5

DRAGON FRUIT TART

MAKES 1 (9-INCH) TART

Crust and dragon:
1 cup unsalted butter, room
  temperature
½ cup confectioners' sugar
1 teaspoon vanilla extract
Blue food coloring
2 cups all-purpose flour
¾ teaspoon salt

Ganache:
3 cups white chocolate
⅔ cup whipping cream
Pink food coloring

Jelly topping:
½ cup cream
½ cup water
1½ tablespoons gelatin
2 tablespoons sugar
Flesh from half of a dragon fruit with
  white flesh (not pink)
¼ teaspoon black sesame seeds
  (optional)

Make the crust and dragon:

1. Preheat the oven to 325°F.

2. Beat the butter with an electric mixer until pale and fluffy. Add the confectioners' sugar and beat for 2 minutes, until well combined. Add the vanilla and combine. Dye the mixture a vibrant blue color with the food coloring.

3. In a separate bowl, combine the flour and salt, then add to the butter mixture. Mix until the dough sticks together when pinched.

4. Wrap the dough in plastic wrap and refrigerate until firm, about 1 hour.

5. Roll the dough out on a floured surface to ¼-inch thick. Place a 9-inch scalloped pie plate with a removable bottom on top of the dough and cut the dough into a circle that is about 1 inch larger than the pie plate on all sides. Gently place the round of dough into the pie plate and press it onto the bottom, sides, and edges. Cut off any excess dough. Poke the base of the crust with a fork to make little holes—this will allow steam to escape while baking.

6. Roll out the remaining dough again to ¼-inch thick. Cut out a dragon shape with either a cookie cutter or a stencil. It should be no larger than 6 inches wide, as it needs to fit in the middle of the tart. Place it on a baking sheet lined with parchment paper.

7. Refrigerate the dragon and the pie crust until firm, about 30 minutes.

(Continue on next page)

8. Bake at 325°F for 13 to 15 minutes, until the edges are just starting to brown. Keep an eye on the dragon cookie, as it might brown quicker than the pie crust. Cool both the pie crust and dragon completely.

Make the ganache:

1. Finely chop the white chocolate and place it in a small pot with the whipping cream.

2. Set the pot to low heat and stir continuously until the chocolate has melted and combined with the cream.

3. Remove it from the heat, add a couple drops of pink food coloring, and mix well.

4. Pour it into the pie crust and smooth the surface. Return the pie to the fridge.

Make the jelly topping:

1. Place the cream and water into a pot and whisk until combined. Sprinkle the gelatin on top and allow the gelatin to develop for 5 minutes.

2. In the meantime, place the dragon fruit in a blender and pulse until smooth. Set aside.

3. Set the pot with the gelatin mixture to medium heat and stir until the gelatin has melted. Add the sugar and stir until combined. Gradually add the dragon fruit puree 1 tablespoon at a time, until your desired color is reached. If you add too much dragon fruit, it could turn the jelly a grayish color. I added about 2 to 3 tablespoons of puree.

4. Gently spoon the jelly on top of the pie, until it covers the surface in an even layer. If desired, sprinkle some black sesame seeds on top. This will mimic the look of dragon fruit seeds, as they may have gotten pulverized in the blender.

5. Place the pie in the fridge until the jelly sets, about 1 hour.

6. Top with the cookie dragon and enjoy!

Dragons Riding Clouds

MAKES 18 CUPCAKES

Cupcake batter:
1 cup unsalted butter, room temperature
2 cups granulated sugar
3 teaspoons vanilla extract
6 large eggs
3 cups all-purpose flour
1 teaspoon baking soda
1 teaspoon salt
1½ cups sour cream
2 cups confetti sprinkles

Frosting:
12 ounces cream cheese, room temperature
2 cups unsalted butter, room temperature
2 teaspoons vanilla extract
5 cups confectioners' sugar

18 Fondant Dragons (page 45)
5 batches Dragon's Breath (page 81)

Bake the cupcakes:
1. Beat the butter and sugar with an electric mixer until pale and smooth. Add the vanilla extract and eggs one at a time, mixing with each addition.

2. In a separate bowl, combine the flour, baking soda, and salt. Add this to the batter in 2 additions, alternating with the sour cream. Fold in the confetti sprinkles.

3. Spoon the batter into 2 lined cupcake pans. Bake at 350°F for 20 minutes, or until a skewer inserted into the centers comes out clean. Cool completely.

Make the frosting:
1. Place the cream cheese and butter in a bowl and beat with an electric mixer until light and fluffy.

2. Add the vanilla extract and mix to combine. Add the confectioners' sugar 1 cup at a time, beating with each addition. Then beat for 2 more minutes, until light and fluffy.

Decorate:
1. Use a spatula to dollop the frosting onto the cupcakes. It doesn't need to be perfect because it will be hidden!

2. Place a cloud of Dragon's Breath on top of each cupcake, then top with a Fondant Dragon.

DRAGONS FLOATING IN LOLLIPOPS

MAKES ABOUT 4 DOZEN (1½-INCH) LOLLIPOPS*

2½ cups granulated sugar
1 cup water
1½ cups light corn syrup
Your desired flavoring
48 lollipop sticks
2 cups white chocolate, melted
½ teaspoon butterfly pea flower
   powder
½ teaspoon raspberry powder
½ teaspoon ground turmeric
2 tablespoons melted dark chocolate

Lollipop mold

Make the lollipops:

1. Set a pot over medium heat and add the granulated sugar, water, and light corn syrup. Stir with a rubber spatula until everything is melted and combined. Then increase the heat to medium high and attach a candy thermometer to the pot. Heat the sugar until it reaches 310°F.

2. Remove the pot from the heat and stir until it stops bubbling. Add a couple drops of your desired flavoring and mix until fully combined.

3. Use a ladle to pour the candy into a lollipop mold. If using a silicone mold, you can pour the candy right in. If using a hard plastic mold, be sure to spray the mold with cooking spray first. This will prevent the candy from sticking.

4. Stick lollipop sticks into the candy and rotate them several times to ensure that they are covered in the candy. This will secure them into the candy.

5. Leave the lollipops at room temperature for 2 to 3 hours, until fully cooled and hardened. Then unmold and set aside.

Decorate:

1. Use a toothpick or a tiny brush to draw dragons onto the lollipops with the white chocolate.

2. Once the dragons have been drawn, divide the remaining chocolate into 3 bowls and add the butterfly pea flower powder, raspberry powder, and ground turmeric.

3. Use these colors to add accents and details to the dragons.

4. Use the melted dark chocolate to create the dragons' eyes.

* This recipe can easily be divided in half!

SKY EGGS

SERVES 1

⅔ cup melted white chocolate
1 scoop vanilla ice cream
Boiling water
Silver food coloring spray
1 cupcake top (from any cupcake recipe)
1 batch Dragon's Breath (page 81)
Gold sugar star sprinkles
¼ cup melted milk or dark chocolate, hot

3D egg-shaped mold

1. Coat the inside of both halves of a 3D egg-shaped mold with white chocolate. Aim for the chocolate to be about 1 millimeter thick. Leave a 1-centimeter space from the bottom of the mold on both sides, as you need the egg to be able to sit upright. Place the mold in the freezer for the chocolate to harden.

2. Remove the chocolate domes from the mold. Place a scoop of ice cream into one half and set aside. Pour some boiling water into a bowl and place a plate on top. The heat of the boiling water will heat the plate. Place the other egg half onto the plate for the edges of the egg to melt. Once the edges get melty, quickly remove the egg from the plate and attach it to the other, ice cream–filled half. Return to the freezer to set, about 10 to 20 minutes.

3. Place the cupcake top on your plate and sit the egg on top. Gently spray the egg with silver food coloring spray. Wrap the Dragon's Breath around the egg and decorate with some gold star sprinkles.

4. Pour the melted milk or dark chocolate on top of the egg. Watch it melt and reveal the ice cream inside!

DRAGON MERINGUE POPS

MAKES 10

4 large egg whites, room temperature
½ teaspoon cream of tartar
Pinch of salt
1 cup granulated sugar
1 teaspoon vanilla extract
Blue food coloring
Cookie pop sticks
20 mini chocolate chips

1. Preheat the oven to 225°F. Line a large baking sheet with parchment paper and set aside.

2. Place the egg whites, cream of tartar, and salt into a large mixing bowl. Beat with an electric mixer on low speed until the eggs look foamy. The mixing bowl and the whisks must be completely clean and grease-free, as the egg whites will not whip otherwise.

3. Increase the speed to high and add the granulated sugar 1 tablespoon at a time, until all of the sugar has been added and is dissolved. You'll know that the sugar has dissolved if you rub a small amount of meringue between your fingers and do not feel any graininess. Beat until the meringue is thick, glossy, and holds stiff peaks.

4. Add the vanilla extract and gently fold to combine.

5. Place 1 cup of meringue into a piping bag fitted with a small, round piping tip. Add a couple drops of blue food coloring to the remaining meringue and gently fold to combine. Place it in a piping bag fitted with a large, round piping tip.

6. Lay cookie pop sticks onto the baking sheet and pipe the bodies of the dragons on top of the sticks.

7. Stick the mini chocolate chips onto the dragons as the eyes, then pip the details, horns, and wings onto the dragons with the white meringue.

8. Bake the meringue pops for 1 hour. Once they've finished baking, do not open the oven! Keep them in the oven with the door closed for 1 hour, until they are cooled completely. They will be crisp and will easily peel up from the parchment paper.

9. Store them in an airtight container and enjoy!

DRAGON TOAST

MAKES 1–2 SLICES OF TOAST

1–2 bread slices
5 ounces cream cheese
1 tablespoon condensed milk
¾ teaspoon cherry blossom powder
1½ teaspoons matcha green tea powder
Pink food coloring (optional)
Gold sprinkles

1. Toast 1 slice of bread.

2. Combine the cream cheese and condensed milk in a bowl and mix together until smooth.

3. Mix 3 tablespoons of this spread with the cherry blossom powder. If desired, add some pink food coloring to make it look more vibrant.

4. Add some matcha green tea powder to the remaining spread.

5. Place the green and pink spread into piping bags fitted with large, round piping tips. Pipe dollops of the spread onto the bottom row of the slice of toast. Use a knife or spatula to spread the dollops upward, creating scales. Repeat with another row of dollops until the entire piece of toast is covered. Place pink dollops randomly to look like a natural change in scale color.

6. Sprinkle some gold sprinkles on top and enjoy!

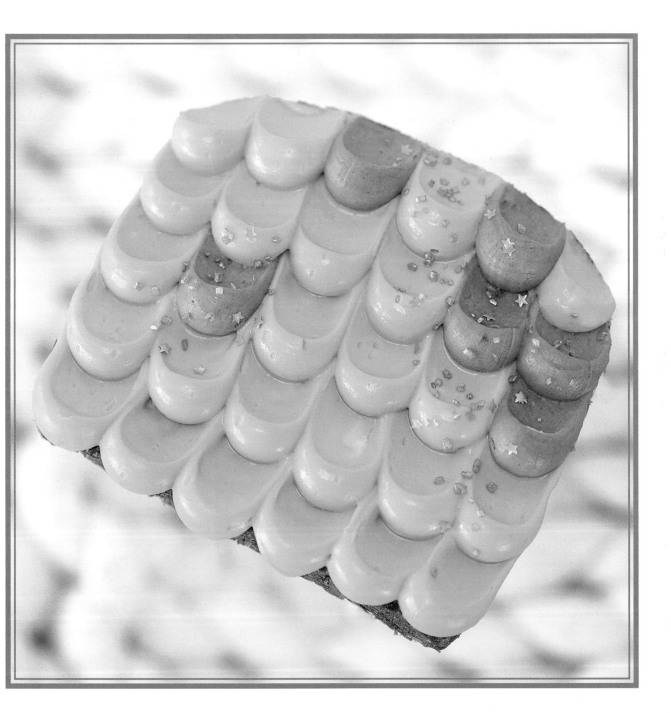

Dragon Pull-Apart Cupcake Cake

MAKES 18 CUPCAKES

Cake batter:
1 cup unsalted butter,
   room temperature
2 cups granulated sugar
3 teaspoons vanilla extract
6 large eggs
3 cups all-purpose flour
1 teaspoon baking soda
1 teaspoon salt
1½ cups sour cream

Buttercream:
4 cups unsalted butter,
   room temperature
2 teaspoons vanilla extract or
   seeds from 1 vanilla bean
10 cups confectioners' sugar
Pink, purple, blue, and black food coloring
Pink, purple, and blue sprinkles
2 candy eyes

Bake the cake:
1. Beat the butter and sugar with an electric mixer until pale and smooth. Add the vanilla extract and eggs 1 at a time, mixing with each addition.

2. In a separate bowl, combine the flour, baking soda, and salt. Add this to the batter in 2 additions, alternating with the sour cream.

3. Spoon the batter into 2 lined cupcake pans. You should get 18 cupcakes. Bake at 350°F for 20 minutes, or until a skewer inserted into the centers comes out clean. Cool completely.

Make the buttercream:
1. Beat the butter with an electric mixer until pale and fluffy. Add the vanilla extract and confectioners' sugar 1 cup at a time, beating with each addition.

Assembly:
1. Arrange the cupcakes on your serving platter. You can use little dollops of buttercream underneath each cupcake as glue to keep them from sliding off the platter.

2. Place the buttercream in a piping bag fitted with a large, star-shaped piping tip. Pipe swirls of buttercream on top of each cupcake.

3. Dye 1½ cups of the remaining buttercream pink, 1½ cups purple, ¼ cup black, and the remaining amount light blue.

4. Place the light blue buttercream into a piping bag fitted with a large, round piping tip. Pipe large dollops as the dragon's body and limbs. Use larger dollops for its head, cheeks, snout, and eyes.

5. Place the pink and purple buttercream into piping bags fitted with medium-sized star-shaped piping tips. Use the pink and purple buttercream to create the dragon's mane and tail. Decorate them with sparkly sprinkles.

6. Stick the candy eyes onto the dragon's face and pipe a tiny amount of blue frosting on top to create eyelids.

7. Place the black buttercream into a piping bag fitted with a small, round piping tip. Create the dragon's nostrils, horns, and claws.

Dragon Nest Pavlova

MAKES 1 (9-INCH) PAVLOVA

4 large egg whites
1¼ cups granulated sugar
2 teaspoons cornstarch
1 teaspoon lemon juice
1 teaspoon vanilla extract
2 cups whipping cream, cold
2 drops blue food coloring
1 banana, sliced
3 tablespoons Nerds candies
3 empty eggs from Dragon Egg Hot
   Chocolate Bombs (page 28)

Make the meringue:

1. Preheat the oven to 300°F.

2. Place the egg whites in a large bowl and beat with an electric mixer until soft peaks form. Add the sugar 1 tablespoon at a time, beating until the meringue is thick, white. and glossy. The sugar should be fully dissolved, meaning that when rubbed between your fingers, you cannot feel any sugar grains in the meringue. If you can still feel them, keep beating!

3. Add the cornstarch, lemon juice, and vanilla extract and gently fold to combine.

4. Line a baking sheet with parchment paper and spread the meringue into a 9-inch circle. Build up the edges and leave a slight depression in the center.

5. Bake until the meringue is dry and beginning to crack, about 1 hour. Cool it completely on a wire rack.

Make the cream:

1. Place the whipping cream in a large bowl and add a couple drops of blue food coloring. Beat the cream with an electric mixer until stiff peaks form.

Assembly:

1. Dollop the cream on top of the meringue. Add the sliced bananas and candies around the center, then top with 3 empty chocolate eggs.

2. Slice like a pie and enjoy!

Peanut Brittle Dragon Wings

MAKES ABOUT 1 DOZEN (3-INCH) WINGS

1 cup granulated sugar
½ cup light corn syrup
¼ cup water
1 cup salted peanuts
2 tablespoons unsalted butter
¾ teaspoon baking soda
¾ teaspoon vanilla extract
Cooking spray
48 mini chewy chocolate candies
  (e.g., Tootsie Roll®)

1. First, prep the wing molds. Shape a double-thick sheet of foil into a 3-inch dragon-wing-shaped mold, being sure to bend up the edges so that it can support about ½ inch of peanut brittle. Continue until you have about 1 dozen molds. Spray generously with cooking spray and set aside.

2. Place the sugar, corn syrup, and water in a pot and stir until combined. Set the pot to medium heat and cook, stirring occasionally, until it comes to a boil.

3. Attach a candy thermometer to the pot and cook until it reaches 250°F.

4. Add the peanuts and stir continuously until the sugar reaches 300°F.

5. Remove the pot from the heat and immediately add the butter, baking soda, and vanilla extract. Mix well.

6. Carefully pour the candy into the foil molds and use a spatula to encourage it to flow into the corners of the wings. Cool completely at room temperature.

7. Unwrap 2 pieces of chewy chocolate candies and microwave for 20 seconds, until warm and malleable. Shape them into the veins for one dragon wing. They should stick directly to the wing. Repeat with the remaining wings and enjoy!

Acknowledgments

I would like to extend my deepest gratitude to my incredible editor, Nicole Frail, whose guidance, expertise, and unwavering support has been instrumental in bringing this cookbook to life. Your keen eye for detail has truly elevated this project and I am immensely grateful for your collaboration every step of the way.

To my wonderful fiancé, Brendan, thank you for tolerating the chaos and endless sink of dirty dishes as I wrote and shot this book. Thank you for encouraging me when I felt overwhelmed and for being the official taste-tester of each recipe. You are the one I am proudest to present my creations to and the biggest cheerleader I could ever ask for. I love you!

Index

Metric Conversions

If you're accustomed to using metric measurements, use these handy charts to convert the imperial measurements used in this book.

Weight (Dry Ingredients)

1 oz		30 g
4 oz	¼ lb	120 g
8 oz	½ lb	240 g
12 oz	¾ lb	360 g
16 oz	1 lb	480 g
32 oz	2 lb	960 g

Oven Temperatures

Fahrenheit	Celsius	Gas Mark
225°	110°	¼
250°	120°	½
275°	140°	1
300°	150°	2
325°	160°	3
350°	180°	4
375°	190°	5
400°	200°	6
425°	220°	7
450°	230°	8

Volume (Liquid Ingredients)

½ tsp.		2 ml
1 tsp.		5 ml
1 Tbsp.	½ fl oz	15 ml
2 Tbsp.	1 fl oz	30 ml
¼ cup	2 fl oz	60 ml
⅓ cup	3 fl oz	80 ml
½ cup	4 fl oz	120 ml
⅔ cup	5 fl oz	160 ml
¾ cup	6 fl oz	180 ml
1 cup	8 fl oz	240 ml
1 pt	16 fl oz	480 ml
1 qt	32 fl oz	960 ml

Length

¼ in	6 mm
½ in	13 mm
¾ in	19 mm
1 in	25 mm
6 in	15 cm
12 in	30 cm

ALSO AVAILABLE